"This book is fantastic!

I thoroughly enjoyed reading it and feel that it will help many people. Although our individual journeys in life are completely unique and in fact Self-Designed, there are many helpful signposts that you can encounter along the way if you simply ask for them! This book can be one of those for you.

A captivating and amusing rollicking read!

Highly recommended!

Thanks for the very generous and loving portrayal of the Matrix Energetics experience!"

Richard Bartlett DC, ND

(Profanity)?!

How I Went From an Atheist to
Quantum Wizard
in Less than a Decade!

JOSHUA RAMAY

BALBOA.
PRESS

A DIVISION OF HAY HOUSE

Balboa Press books may be ordered through booksellers or by contacting:

Balboa Press
A Division of Hay House
1663 Liberty Drive
Bloomington, IN 47403
www.balboapress.com
1 (877) 407-4847

Print information available on the last page.

ISBN: 978-1-5043-4774-7 (sc)
ISBN: 978-1-5043-4776-1 (hc)
ISBN: 978-1-5043-4775-4 (e)

Library of Congress Control Number: 2015921052

Balboa Press rev. date: 2/25/2016

To Dr. Richard Bartlett and Bill Cooper,
Warriors of the Light,
whose ancestral jewelry
require a wheelbarrow for comfortable travel.

I also wish to thank,
of course,
Joanne K. Rowling.

Attempting to describe or explain spirituality to an atheist is about as futile as cooking a 3-star Michelin meal for a man with a burned tongue and sinuses, or playing a Mozart sonata to a deaf person, though I shall make the attempt. How to explain to them that we are not delusional due to their faculties' inability to register spiritual realities upon their organs of perception, or how truly wretched or sad this is, and how fortunate they are, at least in a way, to not feel their extreme loss? I will make that attempt nonetheless, as so many have before myself.

-Me

The cynic, or extreme skeptic, is the worst form of intellectual coward; this way they get to be right no matter what.

-Me again

Introduction

I suppose that an introduction should begin by introducing one's self, especially if the book is moderately autobiographical, so…pleased to meet you! My name is Josh. And you are? Well, that's THE QUESTION isn't it? I used to think that I knew who and what I was, though I can't say I gave those notions very much thought or import for the first nineteen years of my life. Like many of you, I was taught, especially in school, that scholastic knowledge was power and its acquisition the only path available to us all to bend life to our will, get what we want, and pursue happiness. It helped me, or so I thought, that I didn't believe in God. Did I mention that? Of course not, we just met.

What a hindrance, I mused, would it be to climb over endless dogmatic, mythological codices that the world's religions were threatening the earth's children with?! A Creator, who with a Word created the Universe, galaxies, and worlds without end (and All-Loving no less) would arrange to endlessly torture those microscopic creations heralded as His children for non-compliance of the vaguest of rules, hallucinated by men (and *only men*) who would have probably been institutionalized by today's medical/psychological standards?

Crazy-town, I thought. Why should I cripple myself with such hypocritical, fearful nonsense when all I saw in the world was that brilliant, intellectually-oriented individuals guided the course of today's humanity (albeit haphazardly)? I was not a sheep, and certainly no lamb. I sought to be a shepherd.

I'll admit it, I wanted at different points in my life to believe, despite the endless forms and quantities of destruction that differences in religion had wrought, that Yahweh was there somewhere, guiding everything and everyone. Yet there was nothing in the world's carnage, inequity, starvation, war, and control governments to suggest that Allah's smiling face shined upon us. What perfect Creator could allow all this?

So I naturally deduced that it was a load of crap, and that folks worldwide were being conned into subservience, mental control, and poverty because they were afraid of death, and therefore Life. The men running this con, it seemed, commanded endless material wealth while countless believers starved, or lived in squalor, even if *their* spiritual figureheads were penniless!

Well...screw that, I reasoned. I was no dupe. I was going to build my intellect, as I was taught to, and let today's proven God, Science, guide my future's dreams for humanity. Mysticism was for suckers, and useless, on this chaotic planet. Thought and worldly knowledge...King. I was a total Buggle.

(Hold your nose and say it...you know what I can't legally call it;-)

Ahhh....the best laid plans (and believe you me, I had them figured out until the worms lunched upon my decaying form). The beautiful illusions of control and certainty.

The Tao, it seems, had other designs for me.

Hallef-inglulleah and thank Christ-Buddha-Krishna-Melchizedek-Elohim! Thank all Goddesses and Dumbledore to boot!

Sometime during the second semester of my second year of college, I had an awakening so huge, a spiritual experience so vast, that I not only believed, not only had faith, but KNEW beyond all doubt forever that God/Source existed, loved us all unconditionally, and barely resembled what humanity thought She/He was. Ditto for the Divine Sons and Daughters who throughout history, and every culture, have taught through example and Word how to relate to this mysterious yet omniscient, omnipotent, and omnipresent Parent. I'd never been so happy to be so incredibly wrong in my short life.

For the following ten years, my life resembled an incredibly bizarre adventure, and nothing what I thought it would be like. The spiritual revelations I've had, abilities that I've come to develop, and informational resources I've discovered and experimented with have been beyond what my wildest imagination could have summoned. I'm going to lay it all out for you, just as I had discovered them, in the book you're holding (or the digital pirated version you downloaded from Torrentz;-).

It's your birthright to know about this stuff, and I won't hold anything back from you about the experience I had. My approaches to the deepening connection with my Spirit have been fairly meticulous, and would have loved a book like this one at the beginning of my path, to test what it proposes for myself. Open-minded skepticism is healthy, I've found, as long as it doesn't suffocate the will to explore and childlike ability to savor and enjoy the process of discovery.

I name the book What The F---! for this very reason; because I've said that very American phrase so many times in the last ten years during this process, and so will your reasoning mind, I imagine. It's precisely because we've identified *who we are* with our linear left-brain, that it gets perpetually amazed with what the right-brain and heart (multi-dimensional, intuitive information) can access when focused upon. I'm pretty sure you'll say WTF! a few times as well.

The book is about my own experience of these concepts, modalities, initiations, attunements, and growth for over a decade (into the quantum wizard-type I've now become). It's just one ex-Atheist's perspective. (If you are currently an Atheist, wear the same smirk of amused skepticism and doubt that I used to don and continue on for entertainment value if you wish. If, however, this book poses any intriguing mental hypothetical postulates for you, please do have the intellectual curiosity and cojones to research these concepts in a scientific manner as is your custom.)

If you are already awakening to your spiritual journey consciously, regardless of which path you follow, then this book might greatly appeal to you also. You may recognize pieces of yourself in its pages, where the progression of your own winding path has led you to hear or see my thoughts and words in your head right now. Hello.

This is my Spiritual Treasure Chest and Tool Box. Everything I've tripped into, played with, and become in ten years of intense, yet joyful investigation: From energy healing modalities, tools, inventions, Masters, gurus, books, and more.

I am both mystically and scientifically curious what usefulness this information may forge in your life, because the path to God, I've discovered, is an Art and Science, Beauty, Revelation and more. We're all in this together my friend, because we're One (or so quantum physicists are proving through experimentation).

Bon Appetite!

Joshua Ramay
San Diego, California, 2009

Chapter 1

So...I'm sitting in my parents' car at a red light, right? It was an unusually weird day for me, and I don't *do* weird at this point in my life. Pretty much a clockwork path laid ahead of me: Transferring to University of California at Berkeley in a semester's time, majoring in God knows what (though there's no God at this moment) and a job I despise at a bank vault counting other peoples' money. I needed the job because I had to help my parents pay for the exponentially increasing cost of university education and I was only going for two years. The first two (or at this point, 1.5yrs.) had been spent at high school part deux, or community college.

I had enrolled myself in a direct-transfer program as conciliation for being rejected by the aforementioned UC school, even though I had a really high GPA and did every extracurricular activity under the sun. As long as I maintained a 3.0 grade point average at the community college for two years, I was guaranteed a place at Berkeley as a junior. I was bored a lot of the time, but the experience wasn't a total waste. Singing base in their choir was awesome, and learned that I had hidden abilities in acting and writing poetry. I also had some truly exceptional educators, too. I had always excelled in the realm of academia, believing it to be my key to life's successes, yet it was a rare occurrence when I found anything in class to peak my authentic interest.

I knew from an early age that success in school had little to do with actual learning or depth of thought. It had everything to do with psychologically analyzing one's teacher, understanding their patterns, views on their subject, and subsequent meeting of their particular expectations that wrought achievement in their class. This strategy had worked for years, and I found, was equally applicable to community college.

I was hungry to challenge the established paradigms in every field, in every subject, because I had so many ideas and questions, and so many things in this world just didn't add-up. My professors didn't seem to have the desire to explore any further than their syllabi. Oh well, I'd sigh to myself, just a little longer until Berkeley.

I thought perhaps that Western Philosophy might be my saving grace; ambrosia and nectar against the wounds of intellectual iniquity, where free thought could examine every angle of every subject already perceived to be set in tablature. I had been looking forward to the class ever since I was introduced to Plato's writings in high school.

Its founder, Socrates, my hero to this date, was famous and heralded as wisest because he boldly declared that he didn't know shit. He was, in fact, murdered by his contemporaries because he proved repetitiously that everyone else did not know what they were talking about either, even though they thought that they did (my kind of guy). It seems, however, that I had been mistaken.

My professor (I use the term loosely) was under the illusion that the answers *were* set in stone, that he knew what Kafka meant, etc...we argued all semester. I don't believe he

2

was a lover of wisdom, and can you really teach what you don't love and therefore know?

Ahhhh...modern philosophy. Endless, circular, intellectual masturbation with no pay-off or pragmatism.

I'll admit I had no higher hopes when I enrolled in Eastern Philosophy. I had heard of Buddhists and knew of them vaguely as a peaceful bunch. I admired this trait, and honestly, I was miserly with my admiration of anything even remotely involving religions. I was aware of the contemporary running jokes applied often to Hari Krishnas; their funny clothes and music, in-your-face evangelicalism, and cultish surrender of individuality. Though I thought they disturbed the general peace, I also quietly approved of their harmless demeanor.

I realize now that my believing this sect encompassed all that was Hinduism was roughly the equivalent of Hindus assuming that born-again, fire-and-brimstone Baptists represented the more than 300 varieties of Christians that existed, but I was nineteen-years-old. You don't truly realize that you don't know shit until you reach age twenty-five and Life has roughly handed your ass to you a few times...but I digress.

Eastern philosophy was, well...a revelation for me. Whereas the Bible seemingly had endless contradictions, cryptic codices and plentiful fear-filled admonitions, the scriptures of the East were clearly stated, and even more surprising, were psychologically sound. I enjoyed the mysterious hypothetical poetry that Taoism's Lao Tzu had recorded, though it made little sense to my reasoning mind.

Hinduism, I found, encompassed far more than clanging cymbals, incense, and chanting. Though they lost me with talk of Brahma, Vishnu, and Shiva (not escaping my notice,

3

even then, that these Personalities of God were a Trinity), the Vedas' description of the cosmos sounded on-par with what scientists of today were proposing…and they were written thousands of years ago? Krishna was supposedly an incarnation of Vishnu, and Hindus worshipped him the way Christians did Jesus, though he had blue skin and played the flute a lot. Whatever, I thought.

Then we studied Buddhism. Wow, I thought, this is Socrates minus the proving-everyone-wrong thing. Not only that, it was a guy who said (and I'm paraphrasing here), 'Please don't worship me as God or as a god. I'm a former prince (not the artist formerly known as) who realized there is suffering in the world and I sought the way to end it. After a long search and trying every known spiritual practice…I achieved it in myself and attained perfect peace. The good news is *that you can too*. Please don't take my word for it; if you just do these eight things (The Eight-Fold Path), you too can be "enlightened" (know the Truth) and attain perfect peace (or Nirvana).' Oh man!

I loved it! Perfect for an atheist. No talk of soul, condemnation or fear! Scientists always said we only used about 10% of our brain cells; well maybe "enlightenment" was the ability to access the dormant 90%! The Eight-Fold Hypothesis, as I called it, couldn't be more scientific. Buddha actually went on to describe WHY and HOW each postulate was applicable and useful to life *now* and not in the hereafter. It just made so much goddamn sense I couldn't believe it, and I loved it because it didn't require unquestioning faith! Oh man! Thank you Siddhartha Guatama!

I realized that this was the fundamental problem that humanity faced: People feared a hell that awaited them after death. That their "Creator" *might* punish them for things

4

they did or said or thought that went against the rules He might have set-up, not realizing that hell was on Earth the whole time. Suffering in "ignorance of truth" *was* hell. It was here, reflected everywhere in war, starvation, disease, pollution, and poverty. This man who sought no worship (though millions still do) said that he found the way out into the light, like in Plato's The Allegory of the Cave. Socrates left no map, though. Buddha did.

Doctorate, please!!! (Stephen Colbert voice with gimme hands)

Wow! A person, who not only loved wisdom, but used it, and (I was shocked to admit it) seemed to embody it. Could I truly become enlightened as he had? I pondered the question deeply, but with my usual skepticism (or intellectual cowardice...yeah, that's a burn).

I really desired that peace. My thoughts never ceased and were loud and rapid. Always analyzing. Always invalidating anything that didn't make sense to my mind. Buddhism still eluded my understanding, but I just *knew* that the Four Noble Truths were accurate and the Eightfold-Way could make you enlightened (whatever that really was) because I felt it deep within my body. Like when you fell in love for the first time.

This even made intellectual sense to me; that the mind was the barrier to wisdom and truth, if not paradoxical. It made zero sense to the kid who sat next to me in class, though. Not only did it not make any sense to him at all, it caused him downright agony and pissed him off...and coincidentally, so did I.

You see, this kid was a Christian, and I'll be more specific before a few of you get all huffy. He embodied everything I used to stereotype as Christian: Loved Jesus, but feared God (go figure, as they're supposed to be the same guy), thought he was "conceived in sin," and that we non-believing sinners were going to hell (including our professor).

In almost apoplectic frustration, he would debate with and question our teacher on the finer points of metaphysical truth, and I'll admit that the professor was as patient and diplomatic as could be. I, however, reached my limit with the brainwashed ravings of this young man one fine day, and I ground his intellect and belief-system into puppy chow.

What can I say in my defense, other than that I was nineteen-years-old and had had enough?

I brought his attention to every backward, contradictory passage the Good Book had to offer. Kings 2 where the holy and revered Elijah murders 40 children for calling him "baldy" by summoning two female bears to punish them. Genesis 19:8 where the pious Lot serves his virgin daughters up on a platter to the men of Sodom. Every point he could conjure was blown to pieces by cool, concise logic and reasoning.

I never could understand how anyone who was religious would think that they could argue a point, and I mean argue to the *point of violence* with the *complete absence of any direct evidence*, something that can't be substantiated by anything other than one's own subjective experience. Or what a bunch of dead guys claimed was the truth because *they* wrote it down and had generational cred. Give me a fucking break.

I nailed him, finally, with the fact that no one who had written a passage in the Bible had actually sat in front of, learned at the knee of, or even met Jesus the Christ. I thought he was going to cry, as many do when Truth is discovered to be spelled with a lower-case "t".

Even as I felt terrible for his newfound plight, I pressed on (just to ensure we didn't have to repeat this little debate later).

'How can *you* judge? Didn't Jesus say you'd be condemned for that? What if Jesus was just a guy like Buddha who could access more of his brain, and we idiots didn't believe we could too, so we feared and worshipped him? He could have been a time-traveler, for all you know, and just dazzled everyone with his Star Trekkey technology. If their really was a Jesus, though, I'll bet that he's in Heaven right now sobbing his eyes out over the death, stupidity, and destruction that has been done in his name by fear-filled meatheads like you!' (I used to be very diplomatic).

He had no response to that.

It sure left me with a lot to ponder, ironically, and my whole being was buzzing. I walked down the hallways of the school, lost in myself. Everything around me, from the college girls, the sound of chatter, even the buildings had a quality of unreality to them. Almost like the concept of *maya*, or illusion found in the Hindu and Buddhist writings; like the feeling/silence one feels when swimming slowly under water, but becoming aware of it to the point of forgetting your body.

As though in a dream, and I hadn't even remembered a dream for years, I found myself getting into the car and beginning to drive to a friend's house. The implications of what I had said had rocked me to the bones. What if, just *what if* Jesus was like this Buddha fellow? What if he studied Buddhism and became an enlightened Rabbi?

The Bible leaves out a good eighteen years of his life, and his followers did call him the "Prince of Peace". What if this "Christ within" is the same as the Atman, described by the Hindus as our individuated piece of Brahman (totality of God), supposedly located in the heart?

The Kingdom of God is within. Hmm.

What if there actually is a God?

This question crashed though my unending chain of thought just as I rolled up to a traffic light that had just turned red.

Attempting to use words to describe the moments that followed is a bit difficult, but I'll give it a go.

I remember the sensation of lightness, as you experience before fainting or passing out, though I was surprised to register that I was still conscious. The top of my head was tingling a lot, almost buzzing. Then I felt like I had no body at all. Suddenly, I was floating over the Earth and felt completely at peace with reality and myself, for the first time ever, I might add. Just as I began to revel in this thought, and the clear realization that I was *truly not my thoughts* and separate from them (I was watching them like a movie in front of me, strung together like a DNA chain), I saw in the distance only something that could be described as a worm-hole made of multi-colored light.

The moment I observed it, though, I began to get pulled toward it. Fast. If I could have been aware of them, or had time (though it didn't exist here), I would have soiled my drawers. Have you ever seen that movie "Contact," where Jodi Foster's character was being sucked into multiple star systems throughout the cosmos via a machine designed by aliens? It looked, upon reflection, a lot like those scenes. Also, the ride Space Mountain at Disneyland is close, only without the safety-bar, coaster, car, and a thousand-times more intense.

I realized (because there was no time to think) that this cosmos was no accidental happening and that intelligence was maintaining its perfection and balance at all moments, even between the moments. That there was a Source and that it filled and existed in all "things." Yet, it was beyond even its' own myriad creations. The knowingness of this was so vast that I became afraid, even as Love was surrounding and coursing through me.

My fear jerked me back to floating over the Earth in an instant, and I was sad to no longer be swooping through the universes, but the traditional fears associated with God had surfaced in my consciousness. Now that I *knew* that She/He was real; really, *really*, real, I was naturally terrified that I had pissed Him/Her off with my many denials and blasphemes.

I felt, rather than heard, the sensation of amused, joyful laughter. It surrounded my being and overwhelmed me until I felt peace again. Then with the same knowingness, I'm sure, that a parent feels when they contemplate the Love they have for their child or children, I knew that God had been misunderstood. Man had fashioned God into *his* image, with all his trappings and imperfections; but God was perfect, just as Jesus had proclaimed. We were, and everything was His children, and loved unconditionally in a profoundly personal way.

Not gonna barbeque me on a spit for eternity for what I said or did?

The feeling of hilarity and Love increased.

Sweet. What a relief!

So what now, um…Dad?

My attention was brought back to viewing my native planet. There were many versions of them now, lined-up in a row. Each one had a different theme and future, from being ravaged by nuclear holocaust, one enslaved to elitist groups (I'm looking at *you*, Central Bankers!), some ruined by pollution and others destroyed by nature's cataclysms. I visited and stood on each of these worlds, and my descriptions of them will be limited to this: Not good. Not fun or desirable. These were the Earths to the left of the middle one.

To the right of the center, from outer space (or more accurately, inner space) the worlds became almost opaque, and to the far right, Earth had a golden sheen. I visited only a few, and all were progressively more Utopian than the next. For some reason, I didn't visit the golden one. Maybe I wasn't ready or something. Then I focused on the center Earth. I definitely wasn't prepared for what I saw there.

It was our planet, but I was in an ornate, high-rise office in New York (because the view was obvious and spectacular) in what looked like the 1930's. A man sat behind a beautiful desk, but it looked like he'd been through hell and had been crying, his hair disheveled. I watched him slowly rise from his chair, walk toward me, then turned to face and gaze at his huge office windows. I watched as he ran (in slow-motion) toward the center pane, crash bloodily through it, and plummet to his death thirty floors below.

'Why am I witnessing this? Why am I here?' I wondered aloud.

Then the image melted around me and I was in another huge office, though in present times. The relatively same skyline stretched before me, with beautiful view through the windows. Though this time, I was shocked to turn and see sitting behind an unnecessarily huge desk...slightly older me.

I looked like shit. Like the last guy. I watched, in horror, as "I" rose from my desk with a vacant expression, walked around it, and ran full speed toward the office windows.

As the future "me" crashed through the window, I could feel the hopelessness, confusion, and despair. I saw from behind his/my eyes, the sky above me, then the

10

pavement rushing toward me below. Just as my body broke upon the pavement, I snapped back into my physical body, residing within my parents' car in this present day, shaking uncontrollably.

I looked up and the traffic light turned green.

Chapter 2

Whoa. Um...*and what the* f**k?! I didn't know if I was asking God or myself this question, as I now knew something was listening, but did I just *witness and experience my own suicide?!* ¡No mames, cabrón!

I knew intuitively that what I had just witnessed was my future, if I refused to deviate from the life-path I currently was travelling on. Which, of course, felt strange because I'd never used my intuition before.

I knew, without any rational foundation in the reality I would ever again be a part of, that I would have amassed huge educational and personal debt, climbed the corporate ladder at all costs, and lost my and other people's fortunes. Then under the duress of my failures, I would cast aside my life as worthless.

All because I was unaware that life even had a purpose, that *my* life had a purpose. Right then I became consumed by this stunning and warming revelation...that I was here to do something!

I had no idea what that was, but it sure as hell wasn't what I had been doing or exploring. I sought answers. I sought truth (now with a capital "T", even as I was aware that you only receive teeny-tiny slices of it) and was saddened to realize that Berkeley's collective "knowledge" was only useful to an illusionary world; one which would be evolving progressively toward that "golden Earth" whether we believed or not. Prepared or not. I was determined to be prepared.

To me, the dissolution of the world's systems of control and inequity seemed as inevitable as tomorrow's sunrise. However, I realized that I didn't have to go down with the ship, so to speak. Beyond that, even. I'd been graced with the opportunity of a lifetime, for *this* lifetime.

Instead of blindly acquiring the temporary wealth and empty power this world could offer (as stated in our culture's brochure), I would become useful to myself and my species by attempting the once impossible and delusional: To try to comprehend and connect with Divinity within and without. I believe to this day, and have often told my clients, that a majority of men, had they had my awakening experience, would have quit the world, joined a seminal priesthood, and spent their life on bended knee praying for salvation.

As it was, I was stubborn, and enjoyed the company of a beautiful woman far too much for that nonsense. Plus, I had received the feeling that God desired me as a co-partner and not a monastic subservient. I was eager, too, to discover how to operate the buttons and levers of my reality, now that I understood that we all had permission to do so. *We just didn't know it, or how it's done.*

Ye are Gods and know it not. (1 Corinthians 3:16) (Psalm 82:6) (Take your pick)

No kidding, Brother? Well…if You say so…

Hey, how does this Universe work again? I seemed to have left my manual on the other side of the veil!

Ohhhhhh crap, I realized with a sickening jolt. How am I going to break this to Mom and Dad? They think I'm on my way to Berkeley, and have been proudly advertising this to family and friends alike for a while now. How am I going to explain that (to them) I had lost my mind (or at least had begun to see beyond it)? I was supposed to be the levelheaded one in the family, destined for success and hopefully a catalyst for an early retirement. Now, I sounded like a seeming madman, even to myself.

To say that they didn't understand why I was leaving school would be a bit of an understatement. What made things worse was that I, at the time, had immense difficulty articulating my experience, and that I had zero verbal references for describing it. Actually, I definitely sounded crazy, and my lack of Life-planning only heightened their palpable fear of this unexpected psychosis.

Some part of me acknowledged that part of my desire for material success was tied to gaining their approval or validating their massive efforts at parenting, but I wasn't budging. I couldn't explain myself, or what was going to come next for me, because I didn't know. For the first time, I was playing life by ear and trusting Spirit's guidance.

After an hour or so of heated debate, and recognizing that communicative resolution was far from us all, my parents reluctantly granted my request for the withdrawal of all my savings account funds. James, a good buddy of mine, mentioned that he, too, had become disenchanted by college, and wanted to change direction in his life. I told him about my awakening, and to my surprise, seemed to understand. As we talked, a plan began to form.

He had an aunt who lived in New Orleans. James didn't have any savings, so he needed to find his feet and save some money; we could find an apartment there later. First though (because it was way less expensive and we had no jobs), we were going to live with his grandparents in Mississippi and dig the South like Kerouac and Ginsberg. I had never had a fly-by-the-seat-of-your-pants adventure and was really excited to live life in the moment, chugging on Marlboros and writing poetry. Living in the actual and not abstract hypothetical. Living IT, man.

Again, throwing caution to the wind had never been my style, so with my left brain screaming and insisting that I desist, my Soul and right brain smilingly booked my ticket to New Orleans; the City of Magic.

I could hardly wait to leave San Diego. I realize that sounds more insane to most people; actually dropping out of college to chase-down God's hidden wisdom, but I was new to "seeking." (I *swear* that that is not a wizards' sporting reference! New-Agey-enlightenment-pursuers are sometimes called Seekers!)

There was little for me in my hometown in that department, though it did have the world's finest climate (besides Maui), endless year-round activity possibilities, and beautiful people. Great city. However, it lacked the substance, or spice that I was looking to experience, and 'Nawlins was famous for spice.

I'll admit that I was sad too. Over the past two years, my younger brother Jordan and I had grown as close as two brothers could get. He was five years younger, but his emotional and mental maturity almost matched my own because the moment I learned anything in life, I taught it to him. He was, and is, way beyond his time.

When I was eighteen and he thirteen, at night we would wait for the parental units to begin their respective snores, quietly (as ninja, or NSA agents) steal the family car, and proceed to our favorite place, the Living Room Café. I'd let

Jordan drive us there, one-handed from the passenger side, and I'd operate the pedals and blinkers. He loved it. Sorry, Mom. (Yes, I'm talking to you).

At the time there was a small community of poets and aspiring artists who closed down the café nightly. At thirteen years old, Jordan wrote the most inspired poetry we had heard in ages. More amazingly, his writing only improved with every trip, growing quickly by the praise and encouragement offered by his adult contemporaries.

Sorry to gush, but I was and am prouder of him than I can express here. Today, his genius has evolved toward writing scripts and screenplays for T.V. and movies, but he still puts my writing to shame. Ahhh, the student is now the master and that's how it should be. I am sure Dumbledore would agree with me.

With rare tears, we said our farewells and I boarded the flight that would take me to my new life, and consequently, the trippiest set of experiences and awakenings I've had to this very day.

You see, before we flew out, and of course after my OMFG experience, my intuition was apparently opening to crazy levels. My demonstrations and explanations of this information to other people was insane-sounding, ego-driven, and scared the crap out of them. I didn't care, though, because I was now "psychic". More like psycho, but I'll give a few examples.

I ran into a friend of mine from community college and a girlfriend of hers late-night at the Living Room. When I approached them, I saw them shaking with barely suppressed giggles, and I felt sexual energy in the air. So I, in typical fashion blurted-out, 'So who just got laid?' They busted-out laughing and before I could think, I pointed at my friend's friend and said, 'It was you, huh?' They laughed harder in validation. Cool, I thought.

Then with ridiculous certainty, I mentioned that it was at work, with her supervisor, in a supply closet (sounds like the game Clue, doesn't it?). I then continued by describing details about the closet as though standing in the room, and what positions they used. In a flourish, I guessed that it was while on her lunch-break, what her supervisor's build was like, and then described the tiger tattoo he had and where it was on his body.

Their mouths hung open and there was dead silence. Looks of horror were frozen upon their faces. I thought that it was because I was way out-of-line, assuming something so personal about someone I'd just met. I apologized and told them about what had happened to me a few weeks before, laughing that I was just describing the scenes that were popping into my head before thinking. In shock, they stammered that everything I had said and described was 1000% accurate. WTF! Cool, I thought, but me and my big mouth were at it again a few nights later, same café.

A young woman I had known since the first grade and took classes with in high school was standing in line with her friend. We didn't particularly like one another (one of those things) but we had been in clubs together in high school and respected one another's intellects. She was a *pure* intellect like I used to be. She asked politely what I had been up to (though I could tell she didn't care). Well, she asked for it.

I told her what had happened to me, and what I was opening up to. Incredulously, she challenged me to prove it by asking what her bedroom at her parents' house looked like. I told her, in detail that plainly startled her. All I did was describe the picture in my head that showed-up. She walked

17

away believing I was a stalker and wore a look as though I had peered through her bedroom window all her life. Pfffft, as if!!!

This taught me a very valuable lesson about responsibility, and receiving information of this nature, especially as it pertained to other people. *Keep your yap shut.* She didn't *really* ask.

Looking back, it was obvious that I was looking for validation from others because I was insecure and felt alone in my new perspective. Sharing this new perspective had been a disaster so far. So, like my Berkeley mantra, I began to chant, 'Just wait until New Orleans.' I felt like it would be more likely that I'd be understood there.

James and I arrived in the Land of Endless Gumbo with little fanfare and settled into his aunt's house for the half-month. I had traveler's checks to burn, complete adult freedom, and Decatur Ave. spread before me! The humid, sultry air was almost as intoxicating as the strawberry margaritas I was double-fisting. We strolled through the famous flea markets at Crescent Moon Bay, and by the timeless bars and strip clubs of Bourbon St.

From the moment I had stepped off the plane, I noted that I felt strangely light-headed, but there was pressure in my skull too, as though the cabin's pressure hadn't left me completely. I felt really strange, and I thought it was just the jet lag.

We sat down at a restaurant to eat lunch. Our waiter arrived wearing a pentangle (or five-pointed star inside of a circle) around his neck, like the Goth kids in high school used to wear. I understood it to be associated with witchcraft and would laugh whenever I saw a person wearing one. Not anymore. Not in this city. Lots of people wore them.

He had ice-blue vampiric eyes that stared into mine unblinkingly, and I began to notice a strange sensation running up my spine, neck, then brain. *This dude is scanning me*, I thought. I could almost feel him probing my mind, trying to find out who I was, and if I was a threat. WTF! Could people do that? If they could read your thoughts, I pondered in fright, could they implant ideas as well?

I didn't know it at the time, but I was opening up to the realm of psychic phenomena, in *the* city famous for psychic phenomena, grey magic, black magic, Santeria, and voodoo. I had thought it was all a joke until right then. He wandered off, mumbling something about a message he had received on his Oiji Board the night before. Uh...check please!

Now I was freaking-out a little. Every time I made deep eye contact with someone, I felt like I was under mental attack. *Many* of the street-strolling and working residents of New Orleans communed in this manner, exchanging energy or trying to read a person; I had never experienced anything like it. What happened next, though, sent me over the edge.

I remember that we were walking down Decatur Ave. (double-fisting 'da drinks of course) and there in the middle of the street were three voodoo priestesses. This was the first thought through my mind as I laid eyes upon them, because they were dressed like Erika Badu (but in excess of 250lbs.) with extra shaman-bling around the neck, and they slowly waded down the street like they owned it. People moved out of their way like they did, too. They walked side-by-side and radiated energy. We were walking a good five yards behind them when the one on the right, closest to me, turns 180 degrees around to face me, *snaps my picture with a camera I didn't see she had*, and turns back around without a word.

All I thought was, 'Holy Shit! That's my ass. Time to go home.'

I curled-up on his aunt's couch for a week and was sick with fear, uncertainty, and flu symptoms. Magic: Real. Voodoo: Real. I didn't know anything about either when going through this, or their dynamics/physics, but on a deep, visceral level, I knew people could influence their environment, reality, and even *other people* with their wills or minds. *Not* a good city to have this revelation. Please don't get me wrong, the food was amazing and the music outstanding, but I was moving *here?*

My buddy's uncle drove us to his grandmother's home in Pontotoc, Mississippi, and it was mushroom-level trippy in its own way. We moved into their big, broken-down RV that was parked next to their house on a hillside, where the nearest neighbors were often hundreds of yards away. Stephen King would have loved it!

We had no running water or air conditioning, and it was the beginning of summer. If we needed to do more than pee, take a shower, or use the fridge, it had to be before his grandparents went to bed, because all of those luxuries were inside their house! Still, it was awesome. We'd stay up all night smoking ($2 a pack there), writing poetry, or philosophizing about life and spirituality.

There were two ghosts on our hill. One sounded like a crying woman. Grandma mentioned that a young lady had died on the property years ago. You may laugh, but ghosts are widely acknowledged as real in the South. Folks always seemed to have a ghost story, and we discovered why on a few occasions at around 3am.

He and I both got jobs busing tables in a restaurant in nearby Tupelo, and had to borrow his grandmother's car to get there (much to her displeasure). So I bought, using the remainder of my savings, my first lemon-car off of my friend's dad who lived in town. He didn't con me or anything like that, I was just completely ignorant about cars, having never studied them. It got us to where we needed to be at first, though.

We worked at the restaurant for a few months, but weren't making nearly enough to save-up to move to N'awlins, even with our minimal expenses. The car began to unravel piece at a time, costing me whatever gains I made.

One night, James was following me in his grandma's car on the two-lane road that we took to and from work, when I spotted two Mississippi squad cars on either side of the highway with their lights flashing. A single officer stood in the middle of the road waving his flashlight as though directing traffic through an accident site. I slowed-down cautiously, and as I rolled by, I heard policemen shouting, running after my car on foot!

The first officer to reach my window was panting, but managed to yell, 'Didn't you see our road-block, Boy?!' He looked very pissed-off and I'd heard horror stories about Mississippi police and jails. I tried to explain that I was from California and what the checkpoints there looked like with their floodlights and cones, smothering the traffic in both directions.

Big mistake. Six inches from my face, with spittle flying, he screamed, 'Californy, eh Boy?! Well you better learn our laws, Boy! I should arrest you right NOW! Californy freaks! You plannin' to live here, boy, you better get you a new license!' (I really wish that I could say here that this was a cartoon parody, but it was frighteningly not).

I told him that I had thought of moving to Mississippi, but that now I'd changed my mind. Not two days previously, I

21

had meditated (I did this now) on what it would be like to live in New Orleans. Every time I thought about it, I had a bad feeling in my gut. I wasn't happy to discover that the whole city was six feet below sea-level (interesting depth level).

However, my bad feeling felt the same as the thought of what would've happened if I'd pressed-on with my suicidal path toward buying and selling stocks. I was beginning to listen to these feelings as legitimate information, and much to my buddy's dismay, I decided to return to San Diego.

Within a few months of my departure, my friend returned to our hometown, discouraged by the inertia that permeated Mississippi.

Later, he moved back to New Orleans, even lived with his girlfriend from San Diego for a year or so there. He also began to get the same feeling that something wasn't right either, and came back to California. Two years later, Hurricane Katrina destroyed the city.

Chapter 3

Admittedly, I was surprised to feel eager anticipation for returning to the West Coast coursing through me. Okay, not *that* surprised. Nothing against Mississippi, but the humidity, lack of economic possibilities, and racism sucked. If I had to endure one more N-word reference to something, someone, or joke, I was going to fucking explode.

In California, I had grown-up with friends from every race and culture, and thought nothing of it. The state is a microcosm, I feel, for everything America is attempting to become. Often in the South I heard California referred to as the "Land of fruits and nuts," highlighting one's bigotry toward the gay community, or that the residents there were mentally ill. (To be fair, this was before Joe Biden got the ball rolling on Gay Marriage, and America decompressed yet another layer of hypocritical bigotry from its collective consciousness.)

Though partially true (I guess), I began to theorize that it was simply bitter jealously that California has the most beautiful people, resources, and weather in the country. Hell, 80% of San Diegans weren't raised there. *They moved there.* Socially, parts of Mississippi were still climbing out of the 1950's at a pace only someone living in the South could appreciate. Not for me.

Great food, though.

Incredible freaking food!

Good Lord, I can still taste it! Anyway…

The car had been showing symptoms of less-than-perfect health, but I prepared for a cross-country drive nonetheless. My folks had graciously mailed me $300 for the road-trip for food, gas, and motels (now I *really* felt like Kerouac) because I confessed to them I had run out of money.

I was deeply embarrassed and ashamed that I needed their assistance, but I had to leave. Almost being detained in Mississippi was a sure sign that it wasn't for me. Plus, it was cool that my family didn't rub it in my face, they were only happy that I was returning.

I disembarked for the three-day journey with a lot of Joy, and two cartons of cigarettes (smoking was cheaper than eating at the time). Three hours into my trip, as I was filling gas at a station in the middle of nowhere, my car decided to not start again. It just teased me as I turned the key, and then the car didn't even rev. Fuuuuuck.

Panic soared through me. I was smack-dab in the middle of the state, outside of an obscure town, and had *just* enough money to get me across the country; *and now* I needed parts and repair for God knows what. WTF?!

Prayer time. Uh God, I haven't needed a miracle since discovering you're real, and I don't know how to pray to you properly, but Hellllp! And thank you.

Frustrated by my luck and lack of capacity to address the problem, I called James who was three hours away. His uncle was handy with cars, but he couldn't be reached. The feeling of panic heightened. It was getting near sunset, so I told the gas station attendant my predicament and apologized for the inconvenience. He was very kind and told me if I needed to sleep in my car for the night there, he'd watch over me.

Wow. My tension lessened a little.

When I got back outside, an angel was there, next to my car.

An old, African-American, dirt-covered, one-legged veteran wheeled over to me with a smile on his lips and sparkling eyes. I hadn't noticed that his van was parked at the pump in front of mine. He kindly asked me what the trouble was. I told him in a rush that I had no idea, so he promptly hopped out of his chair, climbed (with difficulty) into his huge van, and emerged with an enormous car-jack. Without a word to me, he began to lift my car and then (with difficulty) squirmed his way under the front-end.

I couldn't stop stammering my thanks for his time, and after twenty minutes of grease-covered examination, emerged to tell me that he thought he knew what the problem was, but couldn't be sure. He pushed himself back into his chair and wheeled inside. When he returned, smiling, he says that he'd just called his cousin *and* his cousin's son who were both mechanics that lived twenty minutes away, and who would be driving-out immediately to examine my car.

I had no words enough to thank him, but I tried.

I come from a city notorious for its vehicular apathy. No one has time to stop and help because they all have somewhere to be. An example: A good friend of mine had been hit by a car while driving his motorcycle in the middle of a four-way intersection in San Diego, and no one would pull-over to help him or direct traffic away from him. He had to drag his heavy bike out of the street himself, covered in his own blood, with people actually honking at him for holding-up traffic. This is an extreme example, of course, but this man from a totally different culture couldn't do enough to assist a stranger. Amazing.

His cousins arrived with their tools, and within five minutes of testing, determined that my starter had died. They then offered to drive me into town to the parts store that was miraculously still open (it was late), drive me back, and install it for me. I was embarrassed to confess to them that I had just enough money to purchase the starter, if I went hungry during the trip home.

My angel smiled, and told me not to worry about it.

They drove me, repaired my car, and reluctantly accepted the meager twenty dollars apiece that I pressed on them both; I had just decided to keep driving instead of staying at a motel. As they waved farewell, and choking-back tears of gratitude, I asked my one-legged angel why he'd taken so much time and effort to help me.

He said that someone had done the same for him when he was in a tough spot and was happy to return the favor to another, *because it was within his power to do something.* I don't think I'll ever forget the power of this first demonstrated prayer, his acts of senseless generosity, or my extreme connection with the Universe at that moment.

I still tear-up sometimes when I think about this exemplary human. His name was Carl. I bless him and his family for generations to come. He was a hero in every sense of the word, and my hero that day.

I continued with my journey, filled with intense gratitude, and conversely, even more trepidation about what the following two and a half days might bring. I couldn't tell if I was being tested in the biblical sense of the word, but I was a little on edge by the time I stopped at the Texas border.

The entirety of the next day was spent driving through our nation's largest state. I saw the same scenic background for 800+ miles; low brush and golden plains as far as the horizon could stretch. It made it difficult to stay awake because my focus would haze-over, and my radio couldn't pick-up anything other than country music. Smoking Marlboro's and eating No-Doze, I drove as fast as I could without being pulled-over.

Arizona was gorgeous at sunrise, and I was thrilled to see the enormous cacti and multi-hued mountains surrounding me in the desert landscape. I was glad to have hustled through the hottest areas during the night as the sun's intensity grew by the moment.

Deliriously eager to make it across into California, I had only spent the night in one motel thus far on the trip. My car had held-up really well since Mississippi, but the Arizona sun was cooking it. When I reached the border-patrol checkpoint at the beginning of California's white sand desert, it was over 100 degrees outside.

My temperature gauge needle had threatened me on-and-off throughout the trip, especially when driving over 75mph (I tried to squeeze lemonade from my lemon), but now it was pulling a gun on me.

There's about a 20-25 mile stretch of winding mountain road you have to climb at the end of the desert before descending into San Diego County. I chugged-up that range at a blistering twenty-five miles an hour, with SUV's tearing around me at warp-speed and the temperature gauge needle rattling at the other side of its red zone.

I was nearly hallucinating at this point, so I gibbered at God and even made wild promises that I'd go to church every Sunday, if I could just make it on the other side of these freaking endless mountains! I had just ten dollars left, was very nearly out of gas, and there were no gas stations nearby.

At the last Border Patrol checkpoint (why are there so fucking many this far from Mexico?), I remember rudely yelling at the stunned agent for asking stupid questions, explaining that I looked anxious because I was out of gas and needed to pee, not because I was smuggling Mexicans.

Seeing the authentically crazed look in my eye and hearing my superb Cali accent, he quickly allowed me to pass.

As I lurched into the town of Alpine (quite miraculously) I used the remainder of my money for gas and for calling my folks to let them know I was close. So very, very close. I coasted down the other side of the mountains to let my poor car cool down, and my heart leaped as I began to recognize familiar landmarks. Yes! Thank all Buddhas!

Arriving at my parents' house filled me with mixed emotions. I could see they were happy to have me back, but still very displeased because of my life-course defection (to put it mildly). In no time at all, they were hinting strongly that I should return to college, but I needed to get a job if I didn't. No argument here. I settled down into my old room with designs on getting a restaurant job like the one I had in Mississippi.

The only problem was that I got too comfortable, too quickly. Recalling how uncomfortable growth was while trailer-living and eating one meal a day, I found that middle-class living was *way* too easy. Dad's cooking: Too good.

After a month or two of half-hearted attempts to gain employment at jobs designed to take a person nowhere, my parents invoked the American tradition of teaching me some responsibility. Being stubborn, and a child of my culture and generation, I was holding-out for a job I wanted rather than needed, while my folks footed the bill. That shit was *not* going to fly, as my dad would say.

I wanted a good restaurant job because of the vision I initially had, but I couldn't tell my parents this. They thought I was off my rocker as it was. I reasoned that if Depression Era levels of economic collapse would occur, then restaurant employment was wisest. You procure food at a discount. In the 30's, eateries still hummed with activity as the populace sought to escape their daily plight. Food and guaranteed work. Perfect, right?

Well, not quite perfect quickly enough, it seemed. Eventually, I had forced the limit of their patience, and had forced them to ask me to seek residence elsewhere. 'Huh?' the freeloading mystic in me inquired. I had nowhere to go, but certainly it wasn't their problem. I was a man now and it was time to walk the talk. Damn, Life is a tough teacher.

Thus began my residence in my car-condo. Everything that I owned was crammed into two suitcases in the trunk and back seat. Before I left, I had just acquired a job at a grocery store, and despised it, but it fed me. I flipped effortlessly into survival mode, rolling my own cigarettes, living on Breakfast and Jumbo Jacks (I bless Jack 'n the Box for all time!), and showering at a gym whose membership I paid for a year in advance.

I had a pretty decent routine going for my situation. I even had a little money left over to buy some grass as a treat for myself, as I didn't care for alcohol. Weed had no hangover and the Mexican herb was cheap at $50 an ounce.

It really helped to slow and calm my often franticly working mind. All of the godly serenity I captured earlier that year had abandoned me as I struggled to live. I still remember reclining in my driver's side bed late at night, puffing my resin-caked pipe and recollecting the miraculous insights, events, and creativity of the past year.

Weed did get me into some trouble though. I got careless and was accosted by an officer for smoking at the beach one day. Even in California in the year 2000, all I received was a small fine ($125) but I also received a year's probation. This would have been no problem if the police didn't have to routinely wake me, but apparently it's illegal to be homeless in San Diego. I used to ask the officers where a guy could park his car and sleep in peace. They said nowhere!

Anyway, after a few months of humping-it at the grocery store, I caught the eye of the proprietor of the Outback Steakhouse next door. He said he liked my hustle and offered me a busing job. Cue the angel choir!

I confessed to him that I had no permanent address at that moment, but he didn't give a hoot. I used my parents' address. I quit my job at the grocery store, happily, and worked like a madman at Outback. You could just live on their honey bread alone, and I almost did for a time! I could run on energy fumes at this point, but now and again I treated myself to a porterhouse steak (Ron Swanson-style).

My buddy had just returned from Mississippi, and hanging-out with somebody who understood me was a wonderful feeling. Everything was starting to go my way finally. Then one day not long after...

My car, my beautiful, mobile cigarette-butt-filled home, decided to die forever. I had been parking and sleeping in my friend's neighborhood at that time, and the local police had been very gracious alarm clocks, but as I crossed an intersection, she died.

When I restarted her and she gurgled her last breaths, I just managed to scoot her up a hill (in reverse only, drive wasn't functioning) and into a liquor store parking lot. I was supposed to be at the restaurant in fifteen minutes for my shift, by the way. Fucked!

I found a quarter under my seat to call my Key (who is like a supervisor for the staff that evening, a pseudo-manager) and this woman did not like me. She hinted that I'd probably be fired for my late call because it was a busy night, and I would be hard to replace on short notice. Then I heard the abrupt sound of a dial tone.

My car was dead. I knew it because when I returned to San Diego, another friend of mine checked the compression of the engine's pistons. He and I were shocked to discover that I had driven across the country in less than four days in a car running on two and a half cylinders. Not even four bangin'. Talk about freakin' miracles!

I sat in my car's corpse in stunned disbelief. Job...lost. My home; lost and probably towed soon. Sigh.

Only one thing for me to do then, I thought miserably. It was still daylight outside, probably about 5pm, but I didn't care. It was 4:20pm somewhere.

I couldn't even think properly I was so sad. Sure enough, within ten minutes, who should arrive but my friends, the police. The car reeked of herb and attempted forgetfulness. Double fuck.

One of the guys was actually a "drug specialist" and had a face like granite. The liquor storeowner must have been specific when he called in the complaint. The other officer looked cool, though. He casually asked for my license and ran my history. When he returned to my car, I just burst out laughing, and he looked taken aback.

I confessed that I was already on probation (weed possession), just lost my job, the car I'd been living in had just quit, and now I was going to jail. 'Oh well,' I chortled as I held out my hands to be cuffed, 'at least I'll get three meals a day and all the sex I can handle! They'll just love my skinny ass!!'

He and the other officer started to laugh and he told me to calm down. They talked for a moment over by his squad car and the specialist left.

I was confused, but had *surrendered to my fate*. With a smile, he approached me holding-out the bag of herb and pipe he'd confiscated from me not ten minutes before. 'Here' he said with shining eyes. 'Kid, you seem like an alright guy to me, and if I'd had the day you're having today, I'd get as high as I could too. Have a good night, and good luck.' I just stood there with my mouth hanging open as he drove away.

I found two more quarters under the floor mat of my car, and called the restaurant again. I was psyching myself up to beg, as we must do sometimes during Life's certain low-points, but this time the proprietor answered the phone! 'Of course you're not fired!' he proclaimed right away. Could I get to my shift tomorrow or did I need a few days to arrange my affairs? He was an awesome guy and I almost cried with relief. No, I told him, if I had to walk there tomorrow, he could count on me. 'Let me know if there's anything I can do,' he said.

I called my buddy James. He informed me that he'd already spoken with his mother earlier that week, and she would only be too happy to have me get my shit together at her house. He also said he'd take me to work daily if he needed to. We both were amazed by the synchronicity of the day's events, and laughed at the irony.

Rock bottom...then in a matter of moments, not arrested, the police giving my herb back to me, not losing my job, and now a house to live in and transportation to and from work. Mysterious ways.

Miracle upon miracle. They don't always have to be huge. When events of this nature occur in a person's life, you no longer require belief or faith, especially when they keep happening to get your attention.

You know.

Remembering daily, moment-to-moment, is the only challenge you face afterward. Remembering the gratitude, and the knowing.

Chapter 4

Many happy months were spent working at the Outback Steakhouse and sleeping on my buddy's bedroom floor. Even with his dog's sleeping ass in my face; *better than jail*, I often thought.

I resolved to not only expand spiritually as far and fast as I could, but now that I had experienced Joy on the lowest socio-economic rung, I next would expand my material enjoyment of Earth. As the Buddha had proclaimed so many years ago, everything of this world is impermanent, especially our toys and tools of expression while here.

I felt ready to serve my brothers and sisters with whatever Wisdom I had attained, but couldn't articulate the innate feelings or sensations of knowingness that I experienced. I was at an impasse, though. I had been researching the world's religions and plainly saw the many correlations that had been revealed during my first initial "ah-ha" moment while swooping through the Multi-verse. However, nothing new was manifesting for me.

I read Carlos Castenada's great works, encompassing his twenty-five year apprenticeship with Don Juan Matus, a Yaqui medicine man and *brujo* (wizard) in Mexico. Castenada's scientific account of his consciousness' evolution was fascinating and seemed to mirror my own in some ways, but the thought of spending a decade's worth of isolated learning, smoking mushroom mixtures, and eating peyote to access truth and cosmic awareness didn't appeal to me.

I just felt that it was true for me intuitively, though I do not at all discount the validity, truth, and Wisdom of the Toltec path to God. Don Miguel Ruiz's masterpiece <u>The Four Agreements</u> later completely simplified and opened this shamanic path for us, but it wouldn't be available for another ten years. Oh well.

The point was, though I knew there was gold at the end of that rainbow, it just didn't draw me in. So I just kept researching, meditating, and achieving no greater clarity. I eventually developed my now-habitual stand-by when this occurred: When experiencing a block or doubt, go to the New Age section of your local bookstore and let something jump-out at you. It's a technique worthy of Hermione; I was always a book-nerd and my eyes usually jumped to the titles or wisdom that I required.

Thank you, Universe, for the New Age section!

A blue-covered book with a title all philosophers could love: <u>Ponder on This</u> by Alice Bailey, popped out at me. I was of course skeptical as it dawned on me that this was a purportedly "channeled" work of an "ascended Master" who called himself "The Tibetan." *Really?*

Then I remembered that most of the Bible was channeled, so I thought, why not? The book was arranged by topic, and though I didn't understand many of the terms and references used to illustrate the content, the amazing thing was that my intellect *couldn't argue against a single statement made* by this master Djwal Khul. Even if my mind attempted to disagree, it was back-filled by images and words that would make very possible why it could be true.

That's a miracle, I thought, as I hungrily devoured and pondered upon the *extremely* intellectual, descriptive postulates offered. The dynamics of the Soul's evolution through time, space, Oneness, and Law (theoretically) appeared laid out before me, and stranger still, was described in minute detail. I couldn't wrap my mind around it, which was a first for me, but the often-pictorial references to All-That-Is soared though my heart and mind in a way I once thought impossible. My prayers were being answered.

This new literary gem had many facets and took a long time to digest. It also left me with many more questions: What the hell is an "ascended master," the difference between a Deva, Angel, and Archangel?

Any time I contemplated either my flesh tingled, so I knew that something relevant was there.

What was this "ascension?" Was it like becoming a bodhisattva, or a realized Buddha? I was confused on the semantics, but Ponder on This gave me thousands of renewed spiritual inspirations and ideas. This book kept me busy for months, but I would still need a Rosetta Stone to bring my mental conceptualizations into something coherent.

This gift wouldn't come for months, as I continued my repetitious pattern of eating discounted prime-rib and mastering the art of busing. Hardly a fine art, but I've always enjoyed laboring to the maximum extent of my capacities; it's sort of a thing in our family. My coworkers loved it when I worked during their shift and my boss made me a trainer.

This was especially cool, because you could then help open new restaurants in the county and teach the new staff how things were done. Back then, before a few meat-heads ruined it for the whole industry, you would go and party your brains out on these trips, and get paid a lot. Ahh, the good ol' days of pseudo-debauchery!

A restaurant to be opened in our area was in a town called Temecula, where a lot of wineries and vineyards were located (sweet!). The training was going really well and I was having a blast. I asked a member of their new staff, who also happened to be into spiritual stuff, where the nearest metaphysics store was located, and he mentioned a place called Lady of the Lake. When I got a free day, I checked it out and the shop was amazing.

They sold every conceivable thing New Agey; from visionary art, magical supplies (for ceremonial prayer), books, tarot decks of every variety (cards used to access subconscious information through trusting an intuitional storyline derived by asking open-ended questions and staring at archetypal imagery), and more!

Very Diagon Alley.

I roamed their bookshelves with anticipation and prayed for guidance. Then, of course, a purple book that had gold lettering captivated my eyes. I just touched the spine of the book and it fell onto the floor face-up (this happens a bit with really significant books, they act like lemmings to get your full attention). Staring up at me was the title <u>An Ascension Handbook: Channeled Material</u> by Serapis. I had never heard of Serapis before, but when I turned the book over and read the description, I was stunned.

In a few short paragraphs, the channeling author concisely summed-up the entire point of creation's game (I couldn't disagree!) and the destiny of the human race toward its inevitable embodiment of mastery and oneness with Source (God). That this was a simplified and practical "how to" manual for ascending Lightworkers (consciously evolving humanity), what lies ahead, and even that karma could be superceded.

Whaaaaaaaaaat?! The end of karma?!

This flew in the face of everything I had researched so far, but my spine felt like a lightning bolt was shooting through it and my hair stood on end. This is what it feels like for me when Spirit acknowledges that something major or true is being experienced, so I hungrily bought the book and left the store in a dream-state. Prayer answered. Cha-ching!

To this day, eight years later, it's one of the greatest metaphysical books in my library, and I have quite a collection at this point. I've found information in it valuable at all stages of my spiritual development thus far. It's descriptions of realities' structures and dynamics via quantum physics and energy resonance have been priceless to me. I've played with the consciousness techniques for years now and still feel and experience incredible results, and I'm pretty methodical about my experiments with Spirit.

If I feel nothing, or notice zero changes in thought or physical reality, I flush it and declare it crap. If it works for someone else, then sweet, but I've trained myself to seek (ask for) the most powerful and universally applicable. All Soul-scientists get results, though I've witnessed a vast spectrum of efficacy and power in the many approaches to working with Spirit. Those who access great knowledge or power asked *BIG*.

The most important technique was referenced to have been ©ed or ™'d in another book called <u>What is Lightbody?</u> by Archangel Ariel (brilliantly channeled by Tashira Tachi-ren).

Don't New Agey authors/teachers have the coolest names? I've met and learned from two, named Sri Ram Kaa and Kira

Raa; I'll write about them later, but is that cool-sounding or what? Like spiritual rock-stars.

The technique's purpose was to unify the charkas (energy centers) of the body(s) through the heart chakra. If you don't know what the hell a chakra is, go Google it; that may take a while to explain.

Anyway, this book was almost like a companion book to An Ascension Handbook, giving a detailed description of the evolutionary symptoms one would experience as they ascended back (raised the energetic frequency) to embodying their Higher Self (Soul) while on Earth, the structure of dimensionality, and even more energy techniques. As I desired to know what the hell a Lightbody was (and to end the lightning sensation frying my nervous system), I bought this book when I returned to San Diego.

All I could say as I read was 'holy shit' (which, coincidentally, happens every time you sit upon the porcelain throne!). These two books changed the entire course of my evolution and focus while embodied as Joshua from then on: To ascend with Grace and enjoy the Divine Ride. We're all on that ride one way or another, I was just now acutely aware of it. The only problem with it is, you feel like the only one for a while until attracting others of like perception. Yet at that moment, I was filled.

So filled, it seemed sometimes, that I was full to the point of laziness. I was so utterly satiated by the Universe's response to my desires for information that my mind parked into the neutral gear of reverie. Like spiritual turkey-chemical.

I would do an amazing, needed meditation that would calibrate my energy to the most optimal balance and harmony, with zero negativity as the result of the day and go, 'Yep, that sure works. Whoa! Amazing! Can't wait to share that with folks!'

Then I would put that amazing, needed technique into a file drawer in my consciousness and think about using the next technique to experiment with, rarely building upon the gain of regular practice. Some folks might refer to that as (the opposite of) discipline: To be a disciple unto oneself.

I was like a child on Christmas Day, tearing through the paper covering my gifts of consciousness. I was so wrapped-up with exclaiming my shock and gratitude that each one worked, that I would forget to use the tool/toy regularly, so I of course received irregular results.

I got noticeable results though. It was the first time in my life that I really heard or understood that our thoughts created our reality; that what we experience as human beings is attracted to us electro-magnetically via our thought, or the holographic pictures we allow into our consciousness. Also, that you could change/create your waking reality by imagining something different if you didn't like what existed.

That is quite a hypothesis!

It sounded like the scientific basis for the physics of magic. I had been a bit weary about the subject of magic since New Orleans, but I knew now about the three hues of practice:

Black magic uses the force of will upon another person/s or one's environment to achieve the desires of the ego; employing the manipulation of astral (4th dimensional) entities or elemental intelligence to manifest specific ends (usually always destructive). This magic always creates negative karma (reciprocal effect) though I'm sure conscious practitioners would beg to differ. These practitioners are attempting to bend creation, Source, and reality to their will so they can have their way. How adorable! Good luck with that one!!!

Interesting side note: Both the Buddha and Don Miguel Ruiz (and quite a few other enlightened folks) included **gossip** as a *major and insidious form of black magic*. Just something to ponder: How many negative things did you speak about today, either about persons, situations, conditions, or even about yourself? Whoopsie. Nailed.

Anyway, you can negate someone's negative intentions, or thoughts toward you if you focus on embodying Love, but we'll get to warding-off evil a little later on. Evil's just another way of saying negativity, but a little more sinister sounding, so we'll go with negativity.

Grey magic is just how you might imagine it. The purpose could be well intentioned, but destructive in effect. Or the intention could be selfish, but relatively harmless in effect. You see? Even the description is muddled, but there are elements of both Light and dark. Soul and ego. So the results can be fantastic, but short-lived or unstable. Only the Soul's creative will has permanence as Love permeates the thought.

Jesus revealed this great alchemical key when He stated: As a man thinketh *in his heart*; so shall it be. Not thinketh in his *brain*; IN HIS **HEART**!!! So shall it be! (I should mention that it's possible that the gender specificity may be due to women already thinking with their hearts; Jesus spoke to the men 'cause we need the most help).

The brain, when divorced from the heart, receives grey or dark (negative) thoughts and only accesses 10% of it potential. Jesus described the creative fulcrum as being at the heart! Dr. Joseph Chilton Pearce, in his mind-blowing book <u>The Biology of Transcendence</u> describes how the heart (which are the first cells developed in the human embryo) and the

41

brain grow as a singular unit until the neck is formed. That 60-65% of the cells constituting the heart are neural cells more akin to brain cells.

His work intimates that the neural cells connecting our prefrontal cortex into our heart are the possible biological hook-ups to what mystics call the Christ/Buddha-consciousness, and that those connections existed in us until about the age of 1 to 2 years when we begin to develop an ego and are culturally domesticated. That these neurological pathways could be re-established by mental intent! An awesome hypothesis to be joyfully tested, don't you feel?

White magic is allowing and selecting thoughts inspired by your Soul and Love. They are often self-less, always positive and harmless in application and effect. It's allowing the Universe, Who may know a little more and what's actually best for everything concerned, to be the editor and inspiration for what's created. Freakin' smart, right? Most people would let a professional investor handle their portfolio of assets, but believe that they know what's best for themselves (and apparently everyone else) from their own myopic view of reality. ¡Por favór!

As Lord Krishna hath created us, and the entirety of the holographic Multi-verse, it might be prudent to let him drive the chariot, and stop side-seat drivin'! *We're* the only thing that can grey the White Light of perfect creation shining throughout eternity or ourselves!

We choose, and we choose with out thoughts and words.

This *is* prayer. Spirit has all the answers to all the tests because we create the tests with Him/Her/It! Let Spirit answer all questions because Spirit has all the answers. Duh! Pick white magic!

So...we create our realities huh?

Great, just fucking great.

My mind was a hyper-moving mess because I hadn't mastered the whole meditation thing. Sure, I could sit silently, and let my thoughts wash over me, allowing waves of tingling (bliss?) to roll through my body. Yet when I returned and anchored fully back into my body, my mind had the tendency of revving-up again, and at that time in my life, would focus upon the many things it thought was wrong with the world. My mind was a bit out of control, so my life mirrored that.

It wasn't really going anywhere, my life. I'd moved to another friend's house within walking distance to work, and was renting a couch to live on.

You know that roommate scenario: A guy at work says his roommate really screwed-up and got fired from his job. So the guy's moving out, and he needs to replace him pronto. The situation fits, you're ready to get the room, then the ex-roommate declares that he can in fact stay as room-renter... and you're now assed-out. Stuck between worlds.

Both guys worked at Outback with me, so I thought screw-it. We worked afternoons and evenings, partied most nights, and slept in the morning. The perfect recipe for long-term success in this culture!

Couch-surfing had its simplistic advantages (and obvious disadvantages), but I realized that I was stuck in a cycle of survivalism; there was no real expansion, just sort-of treading water. I loved serving the customers, servers, and my bosses, adding energy to every evening, but I thought I could do more. How do I use the esoteric knowledge and tools I had gained through practice and experiment?

Well, one night at work that question was answered and a hidden talent discovered.

As a side note, I'd like to now give my deepest respect to those so perfectly serving humanity via restaurants. If you've never worked in a restaurant in your life and have only dined at them; a few things you might like to ponder:

It's been discovered to be the one of the most stressful professions or work environments to exist in. Behind the smiling face of your server, to the 24 seconds of well-dressed (often beautiful) kindness from your hostess, to the magical arrival of your lovingly prepared dishes is a mosh-pit of chaos, temporary alliances, and flaring tempers.

If you wish for an authentic archetypal representation of the restaurant experience, rent a film called Waiting. It's closer to the truth of the inner dynamics of the life and business than you can imagine, minus the penis-showing game and the whole spitting- into-the-customers'-food-thing.

The restaurant is like a dance with many partners, but if even one person is out of step, from the buser, hostesses, cooks, bartenders, or even the dishwashers, then everything goes into gridlock and you, the customer, gets pissed. Your anger then is passed to your smiling server, who then goes to yell at the cook or stink-eye the bartender who tells them to f-off. You get the picture.

Someone always manages to get a bit off beat, too (due usually to hangover, late-night college studying, or partying, etc.) so there's always yelling because someone's needs aren't being met instantly: Yours. Servers and bartenders are wizards of timing, but if a staff member isn't pulling their weight, being cursed out roundly, out of customer earshot is the custom. Whiney voices are heard often and everywhere, complaining an art form, all because *you* are hungry *now*.

Cooks are the Marines of the restaurant. Usually (unless you're eating at a fine-dining establishment) this motley crew of warriors will consist of ex-cons, single parents, tattooed smart-asses, and lots of Mexicans (if you live in California). You learn the most flavorful dialect of Spanish here! ¡No mames, wey! All are hard-working and underappreciated (usually); taking a lot of crap from servers and managers alike, and for the least money. They are the business' spine.

The reason they don't spit in your food when you're being an asshole to the server is the usually-butcher-knife-wielding, generally annoyed/pissed-off Kitchen Manager. You wouldn't screw with these guys' money or rep without physical repercussions, hence, the food remains pristine. You, as the customer, are safe to be unkind (I'm only speaking to those few – especially those pathetic cretins who refuse to tip, or tip less than 15%). Try not to be that customer ever! They define piece of shit!

Oh, and only maybe two states in the Union require that servers be paid minimum wage (they usually get about $3 an hour wages before taxes). These folks, many with kids, live and die by their tips. If it motivates you to do so, and don't feel like the service or food was that good, or at all, look at it as an act of tithing to Spirit...it is, more than you could know.

When working at restaurants, I often told my colleagues that I would express these views if I ever wrote a book, no matter the subject, 'cause people got to know if they don't. If you tip less than 15%, you are a part-human and your mother skipped a few crucial lessons in your upbringing. Only those serving Satan tip less than 15%. Just thought you should know. There, I said it you guys.

Anywho, the crew was on the side patio of the restaurant after a long dinner shift, and as usual, everyone was rubbing their necks and complaining of back pain. I had a lot of friends there now, so I felt no trepidation when I just grabbed someone in a chair and began to squeeze and knead their shoulders.

I closed my eyes and I could almost step inside their body and know how much pressure I was applying and how their brain was processing the feeling. It was as though each muscle had a different voice and could communicate what rhythm, pressure, and texture was perfect; like hitting a baseball in the sweet spot of the bat, or the rightness of a perfectly harmonized note sung in a choir.

Instantly, my co-worker slipped into a semi-coma and begged me to continue. The other servers, seeing her face and eyes rolling in the back of her head, offered me five bucks each for a few minutes massage. After that evening, many told me I should do massage for a living.

Not a bad idea, I thought, as I rolled my knuckles into another knotty upper back. Lightning crept-up my spine and into my dancing fingers.

Then the vision came to me. I saw myself massaging, creating miraculous change and relieving pain, earning at least sixty dollars an hour and working three to four days a week. I saw my needs met with excess time to learn and travel. Perfect answer. I could work on my spiritual path while at work (because its easier to stay positive when you control the work environment) and it served God, ended suffering...even if the economic shit did hit the fan, I could barter my skills for anything I might need. Perfect.

I knew this was my calling, but how to begin? There were about nine massage therapy schools in San Diego, but my intention was to attend the most spiritually oriented. For a year or two, I had asked the Universe for a teacher (preferably one with a physical body!) to no avail. That is, until I attended the Open House at IPSB College (Institute for Psycho-Structural Balancing).

I arrived during the last 30 minutes of the event. There were massage tables set-up everywhere in this huge room at the school itself, with signs describing the different types of bodywork being performed at each table. I was amazed to discover how many approaches to therapy there were.

There were three possible paths of education at IPSB: The Clinical path (which felt a little sterile and rote for me), the Asian Healing Arts path (from Japanese, Chinese, and Thai approaches) of which I was very drawn to, and the Somatic Healing Arts path. I found out that soma was another word for Soul. Bingo.

I had never heard of the massage styles in this category. Craniosacral Therapy? Sensory Repatterning? Truthfully, I had no idea what a Swedish or Circulatory massage looked like, having never received one.

Also, enrolling in this college was going way against my proclamation that I patently refused to spend a dime on formal education again. I don't think I had the money at the time anyway. I was just paying for living expenses as it was, even if they were, at the time, negligible.

Some of the programs offered were over ten thousand dollars. Damn, I thought, how am I gonna pull this off? I was sure that this was what the Universe wanted me to do, because as I walked around the different tables, my hair stood on end and I was fairly light-headed (another sensation I've come to recognize as deep connection with higher-dimensional awareness). I noticed some stairs that led to a large loft room and there were two tables set up.

There were two guys performing the same technique, and the clients were fully dressed...and looked like they were drooling. Their whole bodies were rocking all over the place, even though both men were only shaking them from a single foot held in their hands. It was magical to witness, my head was tingling, and my body was pulling me inside the room, begging for a go.

I approached the older gentleman, who by the way, had turned his demo person into a rag doll (now ridiculously stumbling around the room looking for a shoe right next to them) and I asked to go next. The energy of this man was palpable, as though he filled the room, and his eyes were like pools of space. It's difficult to describe a master of consciousness (he would never give himself this description) and hit the nail on the head. Such is the enigma that is James Stewart.

He said he was about to end his evening, but then changed his mind and invited me to lie upon the table.

From the moment he touched my shoulder with his hand, I was gone. I was floating over my body and was somehow aware of the sensations being recorded by my brain simultaneously. I felt like an endless ocean that was storm-tossed and could feel part of myself that remained still, beneath all the motion. As he slowed the movement to micro-undulations, an explosion of gold light erupted in my brain and saw gold everywhere with my now open, waking eyes.

When I was finally able to float back up to a sitting position, I turned to face the now smiling James Stewart. Gold was reflecting in the eye-pools in his face. After gazing silently and studying one another for about five minutes, I mustered the nerve to ask him, 'So...is your consciousness 5th dimensional or something?' With his rich voice he tones, 'Actually, I've recently began enjoying the 6th dimension and let me tell you, brother, it is something.'

Dumbstruck, and without thinking I heard myself say, 'I'm going to be in your class next quarter,' realizing that he taught there.

'I'll be seeing you in two weeks time then,' smiled the master-who-wouldn't-call-himself-one.

Amazingly enough, though never shocking, the James Stewart was right.

Chapter 5

There's too much to share with you about my three-year education at IPSB College, but I'll attempt to nut-shell-it for you. I signed-up for the 525 hour massage certification program (the license was for 500 hours of training) and it would cost me over $5,000, but I was able to get a work-study position at the school doing administration work like filing and recording grades for classes.

I sucked at the job, but hippies ran the school at the time, so they were very tolerant toward occupational incompetence. It allowed me, however, to work at the restaurant in the evenings and attend the first part of the path to becoming a holistic facilitator: Essentials of Bodywork, taught by James Stewart.

At my first day of school, I arrived in sweats and slippers. I felt right at home in the two-story building at Pacific Beach in San Diego. When walking into my first class, I saw that there were about 20-25 zafus (circular-shaped butt-pillows) arranged in a circle around lit candles, and bundles of flowers in the center. Everyone removed their shoes before entering the classroom. We toned the seed-syllable of creation, OM, in an act of self-recollection and acknowledgement of Divine reality to open the class. Awesome.

As part of our training, we had to learn Tai Chi so that we could become aware of and utilize weight distribution to apply pressure to our client's body without hurting ourselves. I picked-it up quickly and can tell you now, it's an amazing form of meditation, especially if you're the type who can't sit still in a yoga class and have to move. To experience the spine effortlessly floating over the feet, and feel the mind yield to the sensorial information produced by slow, graceful movements was incredible.

If your alignment was even slightly off, it was noticeable because you might topple over and look ridiculous. This came in handy when doing massage, because you could maximize your leverage with the least amount of energy used, saving your wrists, shoulders and back. Most massage therapists couldn't make it past five years in the industry because they blowout their thumbs or wrists. I'm really glad that I selected IPSB, if not only for their teaching of body mechanics.

The program was created with the purpose of students passing the National Certification Exam, but also with the intention of healing one's own wounds so that we could be a psychologically and emotionally balanced catalyst for another's change. It makes sense, right? Otherwise it's the blind leading the blind. You wouldn't want a sick doctor, would you?

If you're about to get a massage (or even during the massage) and the practitioner has a lame vibe, trust your intuition and cancel the session: You don't want their lameness pouring into you. Their touch will suck too, plus you'll be out about $60-$100. Not cool.

An extensive knowledge of the body's anatomy was also heavily emphasized. We needed to be able to describe to clients and physicians alike which muscles were involved with a problem, how those muscles moved, and what bones they were attached to.

Educating the client was important to claiming their self-responsibility for the process of becoming whole again. The practitioner did not heal anything or anyone; we simply provided a space or pressure that facilitates self-healing.

This was often taught to us: The clear intention of maintaining one's professional boundaries so that transference is negated. *Transference* is when the client believes that either the credit or responsibility for change is vested in the practitioner. Neither is true, same as for a psychologist. Maintaining good boundaries is what allows us to help, and allows change to be lasting.

We would be equipped with several approaches to a bodywork treatment during Essentials. The first and most necessary instruction began with all massage therapists' bread n' butter, the Swedish or Circulatory massage.

This is often the style one usually will see depicted in the movies or on TV. Oil is applied to the skin, so there's no friction when the relaxing, long-flowing strokes are administered to the whole body (minus the breasts and genitals). You can apply as much or as little pressure as you like (and *everyone* is different) because the objective is Bliss. Oblivion. Stress relief to whatever degree great YHVH merits your reprieve.

The Swedes, who invented this flowing style, usually apply the touch more vigorously to increase blood and lymphatic drainage (for detoxification), but we do slow and melty 'round here.

Everyone in the U.S. is *so* in their heads, that to invigorate *that* state of being would be catastrophic to our desired outcome: Relaxation. Why? Because you cannot be both stressed and relaxed simultaneously, it's impossible. Like winning peace by means of war (ahem). They can't occupy the same space at the same time, and as stress in one form or another creates our experience of dis-ease, it is humanity's oldest form of medicine. Touch.

Sometimes, or I should say often, receiving superficial touch, no matter how forcefully applied, will only temporarily scatter the surface mental/emotional factors contributing to daily or chronic stress patterns. These thought/emotional/postural patterns are held in the fascia, or connective tissue in your body.

This fibrous continuum courses throughout every system of your body; surrounds and lines every muscle, bone, organ and blood vessel. Everything in the body is held by it. Fascia exists in two qualitative states: A liquidy, gelatinous state, and a hard, brittle state (yes, like peanut brittle). When it's warm, it's liquidy (like the scruff of a cat's neck). When it's hard and solid, you call it a knot.

We were taught at IPSB that where a person was experiencing imbalance (knots) could correlate to a specific way of thinking or feeling that was inharmonious. Many times those with a sore neck had difficulty relating the heart and brain's information, or speaking their truth to the world. Folks with hip, low back, or leg issues were usually going through a tough time either with money, relationships, home, occupation, or feeling supported.

All of the areas of the physical body correlated to the chakra systems of the East and what they qualitatively/psychologically represented to the human experience.

It was all covered in Ken Dychtwald's masterpiece <u>Bodymind</u>. He's a western scientist who re-enforced what the yogis of the world have sung about for eons using the scientific method, and personal, self-directed experimentation. Fantastic! You'll discover that science now often verifies the wisdoms of ancient sages, though it just offers a new label and lots of wordy descriptions (which, of course, helps along the illusion of infallibility!).

Back to your knots. To break-up these clusters of connective tissue, the practitioner has to (usually) apply consistent pressure in the direction of the muscle fibers, and using the heat from their tools (hand, elbow) melts through like an icebreaker ship.

It's sort-of like ironing-out an internal sweater that has bunched-up or shortened in specific locations. Any shortening on that "sweater" pulls on the rest of the threads of your body/suit creating stress, and because it's all connected, affects everything else. Hence, the importance of melting these knots, and freeing the body's range of movement. This is why we learned the majestic art that is Deep Tissue Sculpting.

A body and brain's sensory connections are based largely on habit, though, and will many times re-create the fascia imbalance (knots). So, you have to scramble those well-worn patterns to create lasting change, and to re-calibrate for new information or experience. That is where Sensory Repatterning comes in.

The sensations of effortlessness and of non-resistance are a practitioner's intention. Hands, like TempurPedic, float the limbs and head to explore the range of motion (or lack thereof), and gently rocking the body creates the expansive perception of Peace.

Supposedly, because of the fluidity of its motions, it's theorized that this modality invokes the cellular memory of being in the womb; recalling its sense of nurturing, safety, and aquatic tranquility.

At this point in my massage career, I've given about 7,000 sessions, and I've included some Sensory Repatterning in about 95% of them. That's how great it feels.

James Stewart developed Sensory Repatterning as the artful next step in evolution for the Trager Method developed by Dr. Milton Trager. When someone is performing SR, it's often mesmerizing, as I was at the Open House. I'm honored to have learned the art from its originator. I often tell clients when trying to describe both he and his art, that God Herself would wait in line to get a session from James. Amaaaazing.

This was the first phase of my education at IPSB. Learning these three modalities, Tai Chi, Anatomy and Physiology. We would journal about our practice sessions with people who volunteered their bodies gratefully, and shared our insights, 'ah-has,' and struggles of the past week with our classmates. The school was founded with a communicative philosophy of "Express your truth without shame or blame."

A few of the students in class were expressing themselves freely for the first time in their lives, or others shared the most intimate details of their history, thereby giving others permission to do so. It was incredible to observe my classmates bloom before my eyes and delight in rediscovering who and what they were.

As emotional and physical traumas surfaced and were released from our tissues, it wasn't uncommon to witness someone breaking-down in tears, or storming out of a classroom because the boundaries of comfort or reality were being tested. It was an incredible way to learn.

We would hear and speak about the lecture using our intellects, visually witness a demonstration, then perform *and* receive the technique to know it bodily. Sensation, feeling, and emotional intelligence informing the mind, or ego. Realizing you are not this ego, this social personality, but that which is witnessing *through* the lenses of bodily senses. Consciousness.

Another wonderful thing we learned was that the quality of consciousness and intention we selected would determine the effectiveness of our touch. We were often reminded that "Technique follows perception," regardless of the type of touch employed. Some of the biggest healing releases I experienced occurred when someone was simply present and connected; it didn't matter what pressure or stroke they used. 'Consciousness creates the change,' James would say.

I noticed that all of the modalities of massage; from the anatomically precise Neuromuscular Therapy, to the pain-seeking and medical Chinese Tui Na, Shiatsu, Rolfing (Structural Integration)...it all worked. All of the philosophical approaches to therapy created results because at their core, restoring the body to its natural state of balance or harmony was the key, regardless of the system's cultural origin.

It's funny, but folks usually gravitated to the style that matched their personalities. If they were more extreme and active in their connection to reality (A-type), then the often super-painful Tui Na or Rolfing would be their preference, associating extreme neurological sensation as progress: That whole 'pain is weakness leaving the body' bit. I discovered that this is *not* my preferred approach to wellness.

Approaching wholeness through sensations of bliss, as opposed to pain, was my cup o' tea. My body responded far better to the philosophical approach of invitation and space, than forcing the change to occur. I'm sensitive; when a practitioner touches me, I almost immediately begin to release tension there (and because I don't receive nearly enough massage!).

If it's too much sensation, my body will contract (seize-up) and "armor" against the pressure. My body interprets this as "attack," so it defends and holds. My nervous system enjoys negotiation and communication. Hey, everyone's different.

Finally putting my skills to the test in the "real world" was unnerving, but I got the hang of it during my shifts at IPSB's student clinic. It was a little intimidating because there were professionals working there too, but they were open and friendly.

I learned that massage was a balance between meeting a client's expectations regarding what they think they need or is wrong, their expectations of a specific sensory experience (or what they wish to feel), and what you know as a professional will actually be useful to achieving the therapeutic intentions. It's such a crazy juggling act; ego, expectations, results, time, and smiles. One may hope for smiles.

I had a lot of very satisfied clients, and my teachers all gave me top marks and feedback for my preliminary education (thank God). Soon my classmates were branching out, and received 15-hour taste-tester classes on various paths of specialization at the school. I really liked Thai massage, developed by Buddhist monks in Thailand. It was ancient, spiritual in focus, and was like partner yoga. Slow, meditative, and awesome. Then we were introduced to my first purely energy-oriented modality: Jin Shin Acutouch.

Over 3,000 years old, the healing of Jin Shin seemed fantastic to me. It's theoretical foundation is that by touching specific points on the body and "listening" to the imbalance of the pulses at said points along meridian pathways (like in acupuncture), the body's subconscious will actively re-harmonize the pulses/points and then the condition is neutralized.

It's very much like acupuncture's theories of energy balance, but your fingers are the "needles" for the treatment. Sounds ridiculous, but so does achieving balance and healing disease by sticking needles in the skin! Again, you'll find that everything works to one degree or another.

The girl I was working with was lightly touching the crown of my head and my heart. I felt this building, intense energy sweeping up my legs, into my hips and ribcage. I couldn't believe that so much could happen with so little action. It felt like parts of me that hadn't communicated in years were pulsing and reconnecting vehemently.

Oh, yeah! (I remembered with awe and wonder)

Everything in existence, even physicality, is energy/God! I'm supposed to be an energy practitioner! (Buttons and levers to this reality!! See: early Ch. 2)

As with most of the modalities I've come across, its instructors will usually profess their undying belief that *their* system is the Supreme Ultimate. I realized that there isn't room for growth beyond that, though.

Then the idea struck me to **ask** the Great Flying Spaghetti Monster (shout-out to my Pastafarians!) or God for me to be an energy-healing instrument of Thy Meatbally Will, and to find and learn the most powerful systems available in existence: To master them, or begin to, in service to the One.

I've found that to be a useful request over the years: To ask God for the highest or most advanced, whatever that may be. Also, to learn my lessons through Grace and ease, rather than pain and karma. *Try 'em out.*

So even though I got amazing results and had a breakthrough revelation, my intuition beckoned me to keep exploring. In Djwal Khul's (and Alice Bailey's) <u>Esoteric Healing</u> (which is a mind-blowing read), he mentions that of the two major approaches to energy healing, the best and safest way (for client and practitioner) is the radiatory application. What I mean is that the practitioner is "channeling" energy from the Source via the Soul (out the heart/hand chakras) and flooding the lower vibrations of the client with the higher; negating blockages or increasing vitality where there is lethargy.

The other approach of utilizing one's own personal vital energy, or even just "holding space" through which change may occur, can create an unbalancing of the healer as the client's energy releases, or transforms.

As Serapis had recounted, we are beings of energetic resonance; so if we're not careful, a practitioner can activate their own dormant imbalances. I've found that maintaining energetic integrity to be of vital importance over the years, both to achieving the best results and for non-transference.

Plus, by specializing in energy work, I could get amazing results without taxing by body. A lot of the systems of "energy healing" (especially from the East) required the cultivation of my chi, then its application to the body(s). I didn't like the idea of constantly building my energy then having it depleted, then building again. Then I discovered Reiki.

I'd met a guy once that had told me all about it when I worked at a beach bar. He said it was spiritually based, that the Reiki energy came from Source, and that you had to go through an attunement ceremony with a Reiki Master Teacher to access it. Like a cable repairperson that gets you access to extra, specific channels (spectrums of Spirit) to go along with your basic bundle. Anyone can do it, you just needed to be plugged-in by someone who already has access on its higher wavelengths.

Made sense to me, anyway. The dude was cool, and definitely connected, so I meditated on it.

I found out there were three levels to Reiki training. A Level One class was available at my school in two weeks and I was broke! I was barely keeping-up with tuition fees (pleading does create slack, by the way) but I *really* wanted this class. Everything felt like it had been leading up to this moment...and the class was full.

Really?! I was f-ing confused.

I closed my eyes and asked God that if it was right and appropriate for my path, then some major boulder-lifting was being called for. *Did you wish for me to channel this Reiki?*

Answer: That class was cancelled. Then it was rescheduled for the only weekend I had off work, and I received an abnormally high amount of tips that week, so that I could easily have paid for the class. I got a call from the school informing me that someone had withdrawn their spot three days before the class, and I was accepted.

Boom.

Had I known then how much Reiki would mean to my life, my focus, and my capacity to help others to evolve, I would have savored the richness of these many small miracles all the more. My first attunement, my first true and conscious initiation into a new world, was fast approaching me.

Chapter 6

I walked into the class really geeked-out. Late into the early morning, my mind had kept me awake, attempting to guess what an "attunement" would feel like from a "Reiki Master." I tried to be all "spiritual" about it, drinking lots of water and abstaining from meat.

Well, instead, I devoured an enormous carne asada burrito, a greasy, yet delicious cheese quesadilla, and washed it down with a huge Coke (God bless Southern California's 24hr. Mexican food!). Smoking cigarettes all the while, though I had begun to hope for the first time since starting, to stop. Who'd want to get massage from someone who smelled like tobacco? I hoped Reiki held the key for me.

I was grateful to take this elective for many reasons, the least of which being that I needed a niche. Everyone at the IPSB clinic, where I was employed now full-time, could do every technique I knew *and* a mix of other acquired trainings. I felt inept to offer just the standard knowledge to my clients, even if I was confident with their application.

I became eager to integrate my spiritual studies with my bodywork practice, and Reiki offered me the first inroad. If you're ever offered college-program course credit to learn to channel Universal Life-Force Energy (near literal translation of the word Reiki in Japanese), it's my humble and vehement suggestion *that you do it*!

It's like P.E. credit for a bowling or golf class.

My fellow students didn't know what to expect, because we were receiving our Reiki manuals once we arrived to class. It was held in the same loft classroom where I met The James Stewart.

As I removed my shoes and entered the classroom, my scalp and arms tingled. I instantly relaxed, breathing deeply. There were about eighteen students of all ages and from diverse backgrounds. I was one of two guys (as usual – girls always mature faster for some reason). It was wonderful to meet three nurses who had holistic or spiritual leanings.

There was a makeshift altar in the center of the circle of cushions: Huge, colorful crystals and candles, a bowl, and some sage. Sitting behind them, smiling at us all was an attractive red-haired woman in her mid-40's. Her eyes sparkled with depth and energy. Jeannie Kidwell, my Reiki Master.

She had the visage of a fortune-teller (a bit like Professor Trelawney) in her shawls and many elaborate stone necklaces, but with the soft focus of a brain surgeon (or Greatful Dead roadie). When she looked at me, I could *feel* it.

After passing out manuals and opening the class with a color-based chakra meditation that felt very nice, we introduced ourselves and stated why each of us were there. I think I said that I wanted to become an X-Man. Many people said they didn't know why they were there, but that they just felt a pull to attend.

Jeannie confirmed these feelings by boldly stating that we all had a divine appointment to reclaim and reconnect to this part of ourselves; that we had practiced Reiki in past lives (if we believed that sort of thing). Amazingly, when I looked around for expressions of dismay or skepticism, I could find none. Everyone was smiling and nodding. Not so much as a scoff, and it was a full class. Nice!

I loved these folks, and my heart warmed at the thought that, perhaps, we weren't so far from the Golden Earth I had seen for our future.

I could barely wait for the attunement so I could finally "do Reiki", but we had to inform our intellects first so that it could get out of our way later. We spent the better half of three hours reading about the origin of, and history of Reiki.

I could, at length, describe for you the story/myth of how Dr. Mikao Usui (bless you, Sensei) anchored the Reiki energies over a century ago, how he taught and passed on the lineage through the years, but...I'm not going to. There are many books (some contradictory) about the origins of Reiki, and I suggest you check one out.

We were taught that the attunement ceremony consisted primarily of the placement of hand-drawn symbols (by the Master/Teacher) into the aura/electromagnetic field of the student at specific chakra locations. Once sealed into place, these symbols activate and access Reiki to whatever level one is attuned to. It comes down into the crown of the head, flows into the heart, then exits out of the hands. The more I heard and read about Reiki, the more grateful I became that I chose it, and It me.

Before we broke for lunch, Jeannie went over the perennial philosophy of the Reiki path:

> Just for today, I will be grateful.
> Just for today, I will respect all life.
> Just for today, I will not anger or be angry.

Just for today, I will not worry.

Just for today, I will do my work honestly.

Nice, isn't it? And simple. "Just for today" is the important part. It gives you presence, and returns you to the moment. What else could we possibly manage but today? *Living with gratitude, neutralizing the two most destructive human emotions, and out-picturing this thankfulness to Creation, is the only thing one needs to do. EVER!*

That is why I say Reiki is a complete philosophical system: It only enhances one's religious practices, it's pragmatic and useful, reprograms the subconscious mind away from general negativity, and consciously accelerates your deepening connection with the Source of Creation (by whatever name you wish to refer to Her/Him/It).

Jeannie also discussed the many benefits to Reiki healing (I say healing because it's Soul-based). I list a few here:

1) Reiki is forever - Once you are reconnected to Reiki, you never have to be attuned again. You can't shut it off, piss it off, or have it removed from you for bad behavior or thought. It's your Friend for Life.

2) Reiki energy is cumulative - The more Reiki energy is called in, the more capacity you have to channel it. I personally resolved to use it in every conceivable way. If everything is energy, what couldn't stand to use an increase in vibration, especially if more can come in next time?

3) Reiki is harmless - It's **impossible** to misuse Reiki energy and send it to someone with harmful intent. Reiki has consciousness of its own (as does all energies) and can't be co-opted for petty, astral

purposes. Its origin and vibration are of a higher dimensional order, and recognizing Oneness, only harmonizes. Reiki's very essence is synthesis, harmony, and Light.

4) As you give, you get - As the Reiki energy flows, it must first pass through the practitioner to get to the client. Essentially, you get a healing (clearing) as much as the person receiving. *I loved this point*. I really *would* be evolving as I "worked," raising my vibration while earning money. I love win-win-win scenarios!

5) Shields from, and removed imbalanced energies - This was a vital one to massage therapists, I thought. I already noticed the funky energy I felt after a particularly anxious or pissy client. You can actually feel their crappy vibes long after a session was over. Not any more! Flame on! Channeling the Reiki blasted away these clouds and kept my meridians and chakras clear. Lots of therapists quit the biz, I think, because their body and fields are full of other people's crap.

6) Reiki is endless - Infinite supply of Universal Life-Force energy? I'll take it! Being a speck within the scope of creation, it would be hubris of the worst kind to assume that I could exhaust a supply linked to Source and the Angelic realms. At least I don't have to do anything but think about it to allow it in. Much easier than building and using my own prana. *Call upon it constantly!*

7) Reiki is Consciousness, and conscious from its own plane - As it is Self-intelligent, you needn't direct Reiki; it's deeply aware of what is not balanced either in the body or in the aura. If my hands are on a client's head and their feet are the source of the problem,

it flows to the feet. In fact, if you touch *any* plant, animal, or person, it will flow through you into them. Reiki doesn't have to wait for permission, but will respect if the client has a few more lessons to learn from an existing imbalance. The child doesn't steer the parent, even if they think they do.

8) <u>Reiki is real (scientifically)</u> - For those bold enough to experiment in laboratories, Reiki has been videoed and photographed using a special film called Kirilian photography. It records light as it is emitted from a biological form, and the film showing the white light of Reiki beaming from between the fingers of a practitioner in before-and-after photos is amazing. The before-and-after photos of plants, animals, food, and people who have received a treatment are humbling and beautiful. Medically, it's been discovered to improve the conditions of all pathology, even accelerating the rate at which a bone fuses after a break (through the cast). We were astonished to hear that an unset broken bone was the only contraindication (it means you don't do the technique because it will cause harm), because Reiki would begin to fuse the bone at the bad angle!

Still don't believe me? Get attuned to it and make me a liar!

Reiki is used in hospitals now, and as our doctors are treated as the infallible priesthood of today (malpractice suits notwithstanding), then let us not question their burgeoning wisdom. Like I said...three nurses in the class. One should only be so lucky to come across one such as these in the hell-holes we call hospitals.

I have big ideas surrounding the desperately needed changes hospitals and modern medical philosophy in the West in general have to undergo, but I'll save it. I can almost see my family rolling their eyes, mumbling, 'Here he goes again...quantum this, God that, blah blah...' Sorry guys. Gotta do it.

Medicine has yet to acknowledge the Soul, or that energy is the underlying cause and fabric of reality, including all physics, chemistry, physiology, and anatomy. If everything is energy, and the Law of Mind is the organizing principle, then...well you see the possibilities in the future for us all at least, and why we're a bit f-ed in the present. I regress...

As my classmates returned from lunch, we all were stopped single-file at the doorway where Jeannie was holding a smoldering abalone shell full of burning sage. With a few eagle feathers, she asked each of us in turn to turn slowly with our arms held out as she wafted the smoke over us from head to toe. It's called "smudging" and is a shamanic technique for clearing one's energy field, or a space, of low energy. It felt nice, and peace washed over me, and excitement.

Jeannie then informs the class that she'll be taking us back three at a time, behind a shoji screen enclosure she had set up for the attunement ceremony. Out of sacred respect, I resisted watching what she was doing to attune my classmates, but with difficulty. I just had to wait and absorb every sensation when it was my turn.

The first groups of attuned students who arose from their chairs and began practicing on others looked blissed-out-of-their-minds and were grinning broadly. Then she called my name out.

It felt like, even as I was only sitting in the chair, my limbs and head were buzzing and tingling. My spine began to stiffen-up and throb at the sacrum. My hands were in a prayer position with my thumbs touching my heart. Breathing slowed and deepened, as I felt the warm, soft, electric touch of Jeannie's hands on my shoulders.

I can't precisely describe what I experienced as she moved among us, installing the symbols of access that Usui-sensei himself had passed on to others almost a century ago. I remember feeling lifted, and the color green flashing behind my closed eyes. After she placed the symbol in my palms, I could feel them immediately and powerfully pulsing and tingling; like an engine that's finally kicked-over.

My arms felt like they were on fire for a minute, then it subsided into a consistent, flowing warmth. The top of my head was buzzing like crazy.

'Open your eyes, and congratulations,' whispers Jeannie, 'you're now attuned for life to the first level of Reiki. Now go practice and have fun. Questions? Ask, okay?'

I stood slowly with my arms, neck, and head vibrating crazily. I stumbled over to the table where my attunement group was going to exchange Reiki. I returned everyone in the class' shit-eating grins.

As I placed my cupped hands over the eyes of my receiving partner, I felt the warm current passing through me increase dramatically, like when a person rolls off of a sleeping limb. Her eyes seemed to pull more and more energy out through my arms, as though this part of her body were parched. When they felt like they were full, the energy slowed, and as it ceased, my hands gently floated off of her face.

I placed my hands in the giving/sending positions that we were shown in class, following the sequence of the chakra centers. The Reiki was stronger when my hands were placed wherever she had health issues or history. I was sweating a lot and radiating heat, but all I continued to think about was becoming a Reiki Master Teacher and introducing everyone to Reiki energy.

Everyone should do this, I thought. Children could be taught to consciously raise their energy, heal imbalances, and get the biggest head start that could be offered in this generation. Teenage Reiki Masters running around? SWEET! Bye-bye Ritalin!

First things first, however. I still had to practice a lot, channel as much Reiki as I possibly could, then take the Reiki II class being offered the next quarter. After a non-specified amount of time, and if we showed an interest and commitment to the path, Jeannie would extend an invitation for a Master/Teacher Level class. I could hardly wait, knowing it to be a definitive and certain destination that my evolution's ship was headed for.

A friend from class and I went to the Living Room Café to celebrate our attunement and revel in the day. We held our hands over the table, laughing and sending Reiki to one another. As she released my hands, two small birds of the variety that usually stay far from human bodies, landed on our table next to our hands. We were astonished as they hopped to within inches of our cupped fingers and then stood still.

We looked at one another like, 'Sure. Why not? St. Francis, eat your heart out.' When the energy finally slowed from my arms, the birds cocked their head as though to say, 'Whoa, *that* was interesting,' fluttered their feathers, then took off.

Well, *we* thought it was a cool Reiki miracle, anyway. I guess you just had to be there.

I used it for and on everything. Anyone. At the restaurant I still worked at part-time, I was known as the hangover cure for a little while. In the smoke room, my co-workers would sigh as I channeled Reiki into their heads and necks. Relieving headaches sometimes only took five minutes before they hopped-up smiling, calling me a weirdo, and then leaving. *Laying of hands healing.* I was in my own Heaven.

I was also *always* warm now. This was handy during a cold winter, but I woke-up sweating and hot for the first two months. *Not* handy in the summer, let me tell you. I try not to so much as *think* the work Reiki unless I'm in a session with someone during the month of August.

It seemed to all finally calm down and I slowed my detoxification as I approached my second attunement and Reiki II class. Like Tim "the Tool-man" Taylor, I was chomping at the bit for MORE POWER!!! AGHR Ahr ahhr AAGHR AAHRR! (I have no idea how to spell his man-call). Deeper connection! Let's go, baby, it's time for Daddy to upgrade his hardware!

I entered Reiki II like it was Christmas day, and I could barely sit still (especially because Reiki energy has the tendency to channel through your body even before you got the freaking attunements...that whole 'it's beyond time and space so therefore irreverent to both' kind of thing).

The energy kept building as the class began, and we made our introductions. I mumbled something like, 'Love the energy. Want more. I thank you.'

Um...channeling tons of energy here, but if you'd leave your name and a brief message, I promise I will stop drooling long enough to communicate about the mundane later. Beep.

I vaguely heard Jeannie finally get to why the Reiki was feeling like a torrential downpour right then. Every Reiki level was not only a permanent and dramatic shift into a deeper and more powerful dimension of the energy, but also at the second level, the practitioner is taught specific symbols that activated the Reiki to specific purposes.

We had to spend a good bit of class time drawing the symbols over and over so we could draw them without thinking, or even just see them hovering in our minds. In honoring the Usui-Reiki system, it's generally forbidden to draw the symbols for those who are not attuned, or are going to be (though many Master Teachers have ignored this), so I'll just give a brief description of each so you get the idea.

There was the Power Symbol that revved-up the Reiki (so to speak), empowered the other symbols, and had a whole host of other functions. It was especially potent for physical healing and a general elevation of personal vital energy. This symbol, when either using its true name in a mantra, or drawing it in the air or in my mind, raised my temperature so high that I've left handprints on a client's back!

The Mental/Emotional Symbol had various functions, least of which was working on habit and addiction patterns. I was still on a quest to relinquish cigarette smoking, which was going to be a long-term liability with my desire for deeper connection with God, not to mention my "holistic health" practice. What a joke, right? So I was excited to work with this one a lot.

It focused on all of the emotional and mental patterns and traumas we've picked-up while enjoying this human adventure. As there seem to be baggage caravans in 99% of the people I encounter daily, I surmised that this symbol was going to be my good, good friend.

Last, but by no means the least, was the Distance Symbol. It opened a pathway, like an energy tunnel, through time and space to send the Reiki anywhere and anywhen you wished (Yes! Contact Webster!).

In the first level, you have to have your hands touching the person or thing you wish to send Reiki to, or maybe an inch off of the body at most. Now, I could send it to the past to heal traumas, to the future to strengthen manifestations (people, places, things) or across any distance to loved ones thousands of miles away. How would that even be possible, you may rightly ask?

If we had a sphere, like an orange and we sliced it down the middle, *the cut* we just made would represent our linear time and space, our particular lived reality. If you took the cut and rotated it on its side, it would be *viewed as a straight line*, representing Time. Space (as we experience it) is the *inside of the circle*. All of the points along the circle, or moments in time, exist simultaneously like frames in a movie film, even if our consciousness is experiencing them in succession.

All of the other infinite ways we *could* have sliced the orange are the infinite parallel realities that exist. In some of those concurrent cuts, the pain, trauma, or imperfection *never happened*. All of the points *on the surface of the orange, as well as on the inside are* **interconnected**.

With an act of intention, one could hypothetically bridge this (perceived) separateness, and not only connect with a more useful part of the orange, or even the circumference of the cut (time), but can channel energy to any part of the orange. All is One (orange). Time and space are just reference points! Chew on and enjoy that one!

Just to verify it to ourselves, my Reiki friend and I would go to different locations across the city, call one another to know if we were ready, and then send the energy and symbols into the space that the Distance Symbol had created.

The feeling was amazing when she'd say, 'Okay, I'm…' and my body would light-up with waves of energy and tingling flowing through me (sometimes in strange and unexpected places!). Well, I guess *that* works!

Also, at the end of the class, Jeannie taught a little advanced Lightwork referred to as auric cleansing (sounds less spacey than 'psychic surgery' *and* less uncomfortable). This entailed "scanning" for weaknesses, with Reiki-filled hands, in the space surrounding the physical body. Your hands would slowly sweep-over the body until you feel a "something", an area that feels wrong, or more solid, stuck, buzzy…it's difficult to describe without the live demo.

When your hands felt these empty or dense areas (yes, *dense space*) then they would stop. Then, with "Reiki hands" you would sweep aside, grab and remove, or energize the spot with Reiki, and there would be a physically correlative re-balancing.

It visually looks kind of funny when someone does it (I've had it done many times), but now I can feel the physical part of my body that unwinds when my energy fields are worked on. Freaking cool stuff.

Even though it was just the beginning of my explorations in energy healing and modern metaphysical systems, I wouldn't have believed it then, even if *I'd* told me, just how far down the rabbit hole we were going to sprint.

Never looking back again.

Chapter 7

I loved being a conduit for spiritual energies. *Loved* it. By experiencing and practicing all of the time, I realized that we channel energies that affect our environment, other people, and ourselves all the time; it's just that they are usually low in frequency, and generally caused more harm than good. Not on purpose, of course, it was just from not being aware in that moment.

Whenever I became aware of these moments of disconnection, and there were many, I would close my eyes, activate the Reiki energy, and wait for the bad thoughts or feelings to pass. Even though I was channeling the Reiki incessantly, the times in-between could suck, because it seemed to activate and push a lot of my own unconscious buttons. Processing old thoughts, and the useless or negative ones; it felt like I would be endlessly clearing myself.

When studying spiritual philosophies, you hear about this aspect of the path to God (does this word still create weird feelings in you?). Please excuse the borrowed metaphor, but human beings can be likened to a muddied glass of water.

The water symbolizes our pure consciousness, and the mud; our base human, negative, or limited thoughts and feelings. As more and more of the pure waters of consciousness are allowed to fill the glass (It is *always* flowing to and through us), the muddy water is slowly diluted (cup spilleth over) and we experience more of the truth of our purity.

Over time, the glass (you) is eventually filled with only the pure water (Light, Love) of the Soul. Any word, thought, or deed done with one's consciousness focused on the Divine accelerates this process. *This* is evolution. *This* is "ascension". *Hence, the value of habitual prayer and meditation*; the former invokes a greater pour; the latter removes resistances to its entry.

In the great metaphysical book and hilarious novel, <u>Lamb: A Gospel According to Biff, Christ's Childhood Pal</u>, the young Joshua (Jesus) informs his abrasive and often sage-like best friend, Biff, that prayer is talking to God, and meditation is just listening to God. The book is fiction, but this message is echoed across many advanced spiritual writings I've found. It is the primary way we're taught across many cultures and religions to dance with Allah.

Reiki was both yin and yang: The practitioner can send only as much Reiki to the degree that she can get out of the way and *allow*, and the energy is *highly dynamic* because it's nature overwhelms and actively transmutes imbalances. The dynamic (yang, Father) and the receptive (yin, Mother).

As Reiki does all the work in a treatment, and with Holy Force, the Father aspect is at work/play in this scenario, while we otherwise could be watching television or daydreaming.

Well, with me pestering Spirit to exponentially expand my capacity to perceive and serve, our Mother decided to show me exactly how powerful receptivity, allowing, and listening were.

One day at the clinic, a buddy of mine named Jay DeGuzman who is a Buddha in his own jazzy right, tells me he can help my neck pain. He says that he just finished a specialization course at IPSB that is a super-powerful energy technique called Craniosacral Therapy.

Super-powerful energy work, did ya say?

I booked a session with him for a massage (because if James Stewart had God's hands, this guy would at least qualify as a demigod) and told him to integrate with his energy-stuff whenever he was led to do it.

I've found it wise to leave the general artistry of the sessions I receive to the artist, no matter what type of session it is. Just Be the canvas for the best experience and results (but speak-up if the results are feeling hideous to you... massage is never something anyone should endure unless you're into that kind of thing, of course).

The session was incredible and I felt renewed by his genius with Sensory Repatterning and extremely intuitive Swedish massage. Jay's hands felt even more aware than my own (and I mean by *miles*); it was like he could read what to do before it occurred to me. Laying there and floating, when I expressed my admiration and gratitude, he just laughed and said, 'Just wait.' Jay cupped his tempur-pedic hands beneath the base of my skull and closed his eyes.

First I felt this building, prickling sensation in my toes (pins and needles) and then the room seemed to deepen with silence. Everything slowed down in my body, as though it were straining to hear something. Then, that tingling began to build in intensity as it wound its way up and through my legs. It felt highly electric, but flowed like a bloodstream. When the vibrating reached the base of my spine, my body lit-up like the 4th of July (in the U.S., anyway).

Ancient writings and spiritual teachers describe a great reservoir of energy that lies dormant, coiled at the base of the spine, referred to as Kundalini in India. The Rainbow Serpent to the Toltec shaman. The home of the Power-essence of the Divine Mother (Shakti) as it rises up through the spinal column and chakra column, eventually uniting with the Divine Father energy at the crown.

The Ida, Pingala, and Shushumna; these tripartite winding columns of energy are reflected physically as the three layers of spiraling membranes surrounding the spinal cord and brain, the meninges. These membranes are central to the foundational philosophy of Craniosacral Therapy, and a primary focus. I'll get back to that later, though.

The whole point is that I'd heard of this kundalini phenomenon, but had never felt it; like when people can see the hidden hologram in those funky paintings (I never could, but I know they're there anyway!). Now, I felt like the Highlander after taking someone's head. It felt like "the Quickening" looks on T.V.

So much energy was expanding in my heart and releasing out my hands that I couldn't even curl my fingers. My arms felt like energy-fire-hoses; it flowed with so much force that I had to yell at the top of my lungs. Whatever block was there left in a rush, and I became dizzy as I sat up abruptly, shaking.

I was buzzing from head to toe, seeing flashes of color, and felt amazing. My roar didn't faze my buddy in the least. As neutral as could be.

What really messed me up was that while I was twitching all over the table, Jay was calmly describing in detail *every* bilateral imbalance, *every* blockage and tightness in my body from head to foot (and even *inside* my head).

Did it give you freaking x-ray vision too, for Kuan Yin's sake?

'Kind of,' he replied.

He explained that by stilling the mind and "listening" with your hands, the physiology of the client's body becomes aware of its systemic imbalances and self-corrects itself, whether organ, membrane, bone, tissue or system.

'How the hell does it do that?' I asked.

'I guess you'll have to take the class to find out' he grinned.

'Does a bear poop in the woods?'

'What?' he asked.

'Nothing, man' I breathed, still utterly amazed by the most powerful healing experience I'd had to date by far.

Gotta learn it. Ohhh man.

NOW please!

There were three 30hr. Craniosacral classes that preceded the 60hr. specialization. I resolved, of course, to become an expert at it and had no idea how it worked, only how it made me feel to receive it. My session not only fixed my neck, but it was also more open than it had been in living memory.

I was a bobble-head doll after a day and a half of integration. I couldn't wait, and I wondered if I could ever see the body from the inside-out like Jay did. How could your hands tell you all that?

The first day of the eight-hour class (pissing myself with joy and anticipation) was so full of revelation it altered my reality forever.

While introducing ourselves, my excitement grew as many of my classmates expressed their gratitude and honor to study with our professor, D.M., and had heard or experienced amazing things, as I had. Our crystal-eyed teacher smiles, and says that she knows that we've all been healers and had advanced perceptual abilities in past lives, but were persecuted for these abilities.

Huh?

This, she tells us, had created blocks in our subconscious minds based on created fears of expansion, knowing, insight, or enlightenment itself.

Then her eyes closed and I felt the room get still, like it was holding its breath. She makes a few strange gestures with her fingers and mumbles clearly, '74,000 blocks and patterns, so we'll clear that' and every member of our class gasps as a shockwave of energy rolls through us.

'There, that's better' she says.

WTF!!!

I was so amazed that I rudely blurted-out, 'Okay, I want to learn how to do *that*! Do you teach whatever *that* was?' 'No,' she replied with McGonagally-arched eyebrows.

She mentioned off-hand that besides studying with Dr. John Upledger, the originator of Craniosacral Therapy, she had also studied spiritual Craniosacral Therapy at the Miln Institute and was a Yuen Method Grandmaster.

A ripple of tingling washed through me when she mentioned the Yuen Method, so I wrote it down to investigate later. I had a feeling *that* was what *that* was, but she didn't wish to elaborate because it would detract from what we were studying.

Humbug.

Cé le vie.

We withdrew from the metaphysical to the physical, studying the intricacies of the cranium and spinal bone connections, memorizing the names and visual imagery like any anatomy class. However, special attention was given to the three layers of spiraling cranial and spinal membranes surrounding the core of the central nervous system.

D.M. taught that just as a shortening of fascia in the body can cause an imbalance throughout the whole body, this was even more pronounced in the micro-tensions and torsions (twists) of these membranes.

Any tension here could have exponential systemic repercussions in our biology, and does. Dis-ease. Relieve the tension, and the nervous system recalibrates the imbalance to homeostasis again, because harmony is implicit to the body's natural state of being.

Chiropractic, I believe, is completely founded upon this philosophy: That the body is capable of healing itself, given the right conditions. Ditto for Nutritional and Naturopathic doctors (may God bless you all!).

The Chiropractic doctor will use force to create space for an impinged nerve by realigning the spinal column or limbs. With the nerve is relieved, the area of influence and connection it refers to, whether muscle, bone, or organ rebalances its energy, relieving all manner of illness, conditions, and discomfort.

Chiropractors were laughed at by Western medicine for this philosophy, much like they laughed at China when it shared its sacred treasure trove of healing knowledge with us in the '70's. Acupuncturists taught the first American doctors who witnessed the art, science, and philosophy of balancing the energies of the meridians (vital energy pathways that correlate to lymph and neuron pathways), and resetting the physical geometry of the bones (especially the spine) so harmony is re-accessed.

Chinese Bone-Setting (a thousands-of-years-old medical practice) became Chiropractic, and those in medical science who know everything, had someone new to mock. You'll notice that today though, following a nasty car crash, they don't laugh anymore, they just make an appointment. Ahhhhhhh...progress!

This is relevant because, except for this philosophy, Craniosacral Therapy is the exact opposite application as Chiropractic. Instead of forcing the change by "cracking" the spine or limbs, a CST would "listen" with their hands, their consciousness being drawn into where it felt twisted, injured, or stuck, and as the practitioner noticed or observed the imbalance, the body begins to immediately release the pattern.

It sounds as crazy as Reiki, but modern science backs this one up too.

If you rent a humanity-changing documentary named *What the Bleep Do We Know Anyway?!*, many of the world's leading scientists in quantum physics, biochemistry, psychology, and consciousness describe with alarming simplicity how awareness, how consciousness literally effects our holographic reality; as it interacts with matter. Not mind over matter, but *as* matter; molded, attracted or repelled electromagnetically (at least in this dimension).

Basically, whatever you point your awareness at (like a satellite dish) and interact with will begin to change qualitatively on a molecular level; observation *changes our Light-based reality.*

All matter is approximately 99.99% space; this is not a solid creation, it simply moves so fast that it looks and feels solid. In hundreds of experiments, quantum physicists have shown that the form and behavior of an electron changes when observed, versus unobserved. As the movie visually demonstrates, *when unobserved, an electron looks like a cloud or a field of energy, not condensed into a particle.*

This is when it's considered a wave or probability field; or *every location where the electron probably/possibly will be.* When observed with someone actually watching, the electron springs into being and is viewed rotating around the nucleus in an orbital path in a particle state.

So, our interaction determines whether or not we are witnessing (through our brains) a solid reality based on Newton's physics, or its smear of possibility when we're not looking. We choose reality as we go.

Science is proving that we're collectively dreaming reality into existence (as so many shaman have proclaimed), and further, *that the quality of one's consciousness* determines the individual's experience and access to the All.

Basically, that the electron, representing our slice of the orange, is both a shared slice we all share as humans, but has different positions (qualitative manifestation) in it's field for each of us *due to what we think* and *how we think reality works or should be experienced!*

I'll explain in greater detail why this is so, so, *so* important in later chapters and in becoming a "quantum wizard" for this lifetime. For now, though, the act and quality of observation creates changes in matter, and none more so than in a biological form.

D.M. says that she wants to stretch our listening skills. When we progress, she says, we'll be able to feel a human hair beneath ten, then twenty phonebook pages. Wow, I thought, I hope this is possible for me.

There was always this small voice of worry that I'd be the only shmuck who couldn't get it…like those hologram paintings. By the way, if you hear this voice of doubt in your head, I've found it spiritually useful to tell it that you love it, but to shut up. It usually gets shocked at being addressed directly, and usually does clam-up for a bit.

We began with a meditation where we took a river stone from a pile D.M. left in the center of our circle, closed our eyes, "emptied" our minds (if that was even possible) and tried to "listen" to it's journey here.

Crap, I worried, I can't even see the damn holograms in the paintings, but I'll give it a go anyway. Instead of my usual rapid mental experience, I shut my inner mouth and waited for...God knows what?

Right when I was about to give-up and prepare a good bullshit story for my Divination class...a story of sorts unfolded in my mind. I felt tremendous pressure on all sides of my body, and a newness - a freshness surrounded me. Then incredible acceleration as I was propelled from a volcano's depths to be individuated. Endless years passing...my form being shaped by cool river waters. Now, I was smooth and porous, carrying the energy of the birth and the journey, and held in the second human palm to ever make contact with it, now existing in a classroom in San Diego.

Wow, did I just really hear a stone? Was I stoned? Then I remembered those crazily intuitive evenings at the Living Room Café. Sure, why not? When I expressed this vision to the class, D.M. smiled and nodded as though I weren't completely delusional (a recent first for me).

I was surprised that everyone in class had heard their stone too. No one had that guilty vibe of 'I'm B.S.ing this so I don't feel stupid.' On the contrary, everyone appeared to be viewing their stone with obvious reverence.

Call Pet-Rock Inc., I think we can make a comeback!

Before we broke for lunch, the professor announces that she wants to teach each person how to "listen in neutral" so we could "hold space" for change. In front of the whole class. Lovely. Great. (I love you, ego, but please clam-up).

She explains that with this art, the less you do, the more that happens. To achieve neutral hands for feeling/listening, we were taught to relax them and empty them. I just imagined them as mere outlines of hands and wrists; like they were invisible stethoscopes, but still present. It was a challenge for me because I now had a deeply ingrained habit of sending as much energy as I could.

Before we could leave, we each in turn put our hands on her palms so she could feel if our hands were neutral, sending, or pulling energy. I had to ask the Reiki to not flow, and it took a few tries, but I finally got the knack of "neutral" as I began to feel our pulses, skin temperature, texture, and my thoughts simultaneously without identifying with any of it.

It felt like diffusing your awareness so you can hear a single player or instrument in an enormous orchestra, but the information finds you instead of having to search for it. Or, like "spacing-out" mentally, but consciously witnessing what the awareness, especially in the hands, notices.

We all returned from lunch elated and excited for the next block of instruction. Our confidence with what we were feeling was slowly beginning to creep out of the "Major Doubt" territory; but we didn't know yet what to feel for.

Moving forward, I learned while studying about Craniosacral's discovery by Dr. John Upledger, that it all begins with the cerebral-spinal fluid (CSF) that bathes the brain and spinal cord. It's production and subsequent re-absorption in the vaults of the brain was what it was all about (at least in this class).

Every 45 seconds or so, our brains flood the periphery of the central nervous system after producing CSF. When this happens, the primary meninges that line the skull and anchor the brain to it subtly expand, gently moving the cranial bones at their sutures. Even our cranial bones subtly move! They "rock" or rotate, in a particular way and direction (when there's no head tension) in *flexion*, or when the CSF is produced. The bones "rock" back in *extension*, or when the CSF is re-absorbed in the brain vaults.

There's gonna be a test on this stuff later, by the way.

In between these cycles, the magic of biological self-correction occurs. The out-pictured silence I felt during my Craniosacral session, before I released like crazy, was actually this internal phenomenon. This stillness before the CSF cycle resumes was discovered by Dr. Andrew Still and is still called a "Still-point" (wanted to see if I could fit 4 still's in a sentence!). In this sacred space and during these moments, the body's living intelligence recalibrates and renews itself.

You know that time, right before you're about to fall asleep, when you can feel your legs pulsing or tingling, or maybe muscles in your shoulder or neck twitch? Well, I learned that *that* is because your intellectual consciousness that keeps these patterns alive in the body due to habit is beginning to recede in presence, and your body eagerly releases as much crap as it can while the persona dreams.

That is, I think, why we heal so much while we sleep; we're out of the freaking way! It happens during our waking hours too, but we're usually not aware of it because we're rarely *still* enough to experience it.

Craniosacral essentially, through holding this empty space, induces the body into numerous and exponentially unfolding Still-points. That's a lot of twitching and balancing, let me tell you!

This primal rhythm is what we track as practitioners. If any area of the spine or head is injured or misaligned, it will interrupt the flow of this CSF, and your hands notice and feel it. Hell, they didn't notice, they were ridiculously tractor-beamed into wherever there was an imbalance!

It was like, wherever I placed my empty hand would suck me into the body there like a magnetic force, then I'd notice these crazy sensations under my palms, and when my hand finally floated off of the area, it was done. You could put your hand back in the exact same spot and no suction.

Not unlike "scanning" for imbalances in the aura using Reiki, my hands seemed to quickly develop a sense of detecting "wrongness" (if Heinlein and the Man from Mars may forgive me) and when that "wrongness" had changed, or was done with me.

The first time I "got it," I was cradling the skull of one of my classmates in one hand, and her sacrum (look it up) in the other. We were supposed to be listening to the ebb and flow rhythm of the spine as the CSF was produced and reabsorbed, rocking the whole spine back and forth.

Her sacrum drew my attention because it was flat and hard as wood. Also, because of where my palm was, it felt like it angled to the left. Just as I made these very observations, the tailbone and sacrum began to move. By move, I mean throb, twitch, bubbling and rolling simultaneously; her legs and feet twitching as though running electric current.

Her sacrum pulled me in further and my hand started to hurt. D.M. sensed it, came over and said, 'Let your hands empty further, hold bigger space, and just let the sensations be intense if they must. It'll pass.'

Well, it got a lot more intense, as I felt the sensations of movement progress up her spinal column and literally felt the inside of her spine unwind (like there were tubes that ran through the center of the vertebrae) and clunk into place. It almost felt like I was in a tunnel space, and I *saw* the part of the tunnel that felt out of alignment move *exactly the same* and *at the same time* as when I observed the correction in my palm.

WTF!

I quietly asked her (my table-partner) if she felt those movements, and she moaned, 'I'm still feeling it! Now my head is throbbing.' As I listened/looked at my other hand, I felt both ends of her body connect...and light-up like a Rockefeller Center Christmas tree.

She became rigid as a board, as an ocean rushed through tributaries of her spinal canal that hadn't been open for years, possibly since birth. D.M. informed the class how many of our unconscious patterns are impressed upon us via the trauma of *being born itself*, because our bones haven't become ossified (solidified boniness) yet, particularly the skull bones. It takes months for the skull to become a solid, brain-protecting apparatus.

For example, if you had a forceps-assisted delivery (they take the salad tongs, grab the sides of your impressionable head, and extract you from Eden), chances are your temporal bones on the sides of your cranium are compressed. The restricted movement causes neck and lower back pain (because these head bones are connected energetically to your hip bones – if one is restricted, it affects the "rocking" of it's lower-body correlative, causing imbalances).

A sensation I can only describe as Peace existed between my hands, and I felt the suction in my palms stop and release me from contact, even though they were under her body. The body was through with me there. I did it! Or, I should say, I performed the technique correctly...her body actually did it. Receptive witnessing was an incredibly powerful catalyst for change, as so many spiritual scientists have proclaimed for eons.

We rotated partners and I had to work with D.M.'s aide for the class, Mandy McGaw, who was known around IPSB as being highly intuitive. Oh man, now I *really* gotta get this right. I was nervous as hell that she'd tell me I *was* deluding myself, but as I registered this inner doubt, I noticed that my eyes were locked on her shoulder and nothing else seemed to exist.

We were still supposed to be listening to the spine, but Mandy's shoulder was calling me as clearly as those muscles were on the Outback Steakhouse patio. Without a word, I just rested a cupped hand on her shoulder and encircled my other fingers around her wrist.

She smiled through closed eyes and said, 'Exactly! Now tell me out-loud, what do you notice?' Her whole arm felt twisted inward toward her body, like a towel that had been wrung in the that direction. As I told her this, her arm immediately swelled, shuddered, and uncoiled like a snake in my hands; her shoulder, forearm muscles, and fingers twitching.

'You think?!' she offered through a contorted facial expression.

'That was a big one. You did that perfectly. Did you see it unwind in your hands?' I did, but while it was changing, my attention was drawn to her other shoulder blade and I could have sworn that it had let go too. 'I was watching inside my body while you were listening, and my other shoulder blade did let go. The pattern was broader than just the arm. I can see you're going to be great at this.'

Thanks to encouraging people like Mandy the whole world-wide, we are able to overcome our voices of doubt and encompass more of what we are and can become. She told me I'd be good at it, so I lived into that.

We can convince ourselves of anything, but when it's a positive thing validated by an outside source, it makes it all the easier and more joyful somehow. Deciding I'd be great at Craniosacral Therapy was extremely helpful in progressing through the more expansive and unorthodox applications of neutrally held space...and I mean *freaking unorthodox*!

In the second CST class, the focus was on the sphenoid and hard palate, not to mention the many intricate articulations to them inside the head. We had to wear latex gloves as we unwound tensions in the teeth and jaw (dentistry trauma in particular), the tongue, and the tiny bones of the inner skull. It was *really* intense to receive because whatever was unwinding was so close to the brain. Intense.

This class really stretched our perceptual range, because bones like the vomer and ethmoid bone are internally located. We were told to place a latex-gloved finger on the roof of our partner's mouth, and listen "energetically." When I focused my neutral attention an inch away from my finger, sure enough, I felt the vomer's pointy tip rocking against it as though it were physically touching.

When my awareness made deeper contact, it stopped rocking, shuddered, and I felt my partner's cranium release on the sides, like they were release hatches being opened. He looked up yawning and smiling. 'Man, my ears just popped and my hips are vibrating! I didn't know my head was so damn tight!' All from one little bone that may have been compressed during birth. Amazing.

Despite the drool-covered fingers, the second level of instruction was incredible. We learned even deeper energetic or spiritual correlations to the different bones, organs, chakras, tissues, and qualities of consciousness. It all made perfect sense and matched my earlier explorations in metaphysics.

The seven major endocrine glands were the seven chakras; their hormonal dispersion is the interplay of emotional, mental, and spiritual forces out-pictured biochemically. Yogis or masters with an awakened 3rd eye (pituitary gland) would likely see this as colored light, interchanging in the aura. It's all the same.

I was getting amazing results at the clinic when the clients would actually allow me to attempt the technique. Usually, I'd casually suggest doing it in the last five minutes of the session, or on my time, after the massage was over.

If a client wants a massage, they want a massage. They want the sensory experience, *and* the results they come-in expecting. It's a little like people telling their doctor that they know which pill or treatments they want (sigh).

The thing was, Craniosacral created about ten times the results as massage did, but there was no manual manipulation of muscles or bones. It's an internal experience that rolls to the periphery, but an impatient ego is effective at distracting the client from this deeper release, and will insist on an external pressure or sensation to "stimulate the change." This isn't really so; you're merely trading the pizza for the crust. Change is always happening. We're in the way.

I've often begged clients, 'Pleeeease let me do the work that I specialize in. You'll address your issues ten times as quickly, the results are far more permanent, and when you're no longer in chronic pain, *then* we'll appease your nervous system and do feel-good massage, okay? If you do this in reverse, if we do it *your* way, it might cost you a small fortune and the results will not last as long because you aren't changing the issue at it's root level.'

Swedish massage sure feels good, but if your body is messed up and in a lot of pain, then it's a little bit like putting a band-aid on a bullet wound.

Letting go of preconceived notions about what has to occur, whether it be in a healing session, a relationship, or the bounty Life gifts us in general, has proven to be a highly effective approach for my consciousness. As the Buddha said, all suffering (disease, poverty, ignorance of Love) is caused by *attachment*. If you're attached to what shows-up in reality, you will, probably, have to endure a little longer and feel disappointment one more time.

Not being attached to what arrived visually, for me, seemed to be the key to doing (or I should say, allowing) Craniosacral Therapy. D.M. taught that you can notice what's going on in the client by feeling sensations in your own body while holding a neutral state. Also, that you can broaden the senses to "see" inside their body, or a pictorial representation of them in front of you or in your head.

I preferred the latter method of noticing imbalances (why the *hell* should I feel *their* pain in *my* body if I don't have to?!). All of the advanced practitioners seemed to have the ability to just look and know what was off with a person's body. This is what I desired to learn and master.

I didn't achieve this miraculous perceptual transformation until Craniosacral 3: The Amazing Brain. It *was* amazing. After learning about the energetic correlations that every part of the reptilian, limbic (emotional), and cerebral cortexes had to consciousness and processing data, we paired-up and explored one another's brains. BRRAAAAINS!!!

When I touched my partner's head and closed my eyes, I was sucked inside her skull like a victim's bullet path in a CSI: Miami show. I was standing inside her brain (in the upper vaults where the CSF is produced), and everywhere I looked, I could see the various structures of it in vivid detail right in front of me.

As I neutrally observed the imbalances or tensions in her brain stem, I observed it relax, unwind, and witnessed the release spiral down to the bottom of her spine. I knew her sacrum had released, so I kept looking around.

Everything was releasing; I could see every tension in her head and could feel her twitching in my hands.

When I opened my eyes, it was like I was still inside her cranium. I could focus my neutral gaze wherever my attention was drawn first, and like x-ray (but better) could "see" where the tension was and how it ran through the body. It helped a great deal that I knew the anatomy of the body, how things connected or flowed. The many layers, structures, and systems were my "hologram in the painting," but I could actually visualize this!

Afterward, using a huge wall diagram of its internal structures, we were asked to describe what our partner's brain was like and how it shifted. In a rush of excitement, I recalled in detail the state of every structure of her brain with more confidence than I'd ever had.

I think looking back, that my teacher thought I was trying to show-off this new break-through, but I didn't care *because she confirmed every observation I made!* I could *see*, or at least I was beginning to.

I'll have to admit here that I couldn't really conceive of anything cooler than learning how to tune-in or listen to someone's body, see the pattern melt from the inside in crazy Technicolor, then energize the area with some Reiki.

I mean, if this is all you did, you could take your human experience for this life and deem it well spent, both for personal cultivation and public contribution.

However...

That habit of always asking Spirit for the most powerful, most advanced, deepest accessing, and evolution-accelerating techniques and energy systems available to humanity never deactivated in me.

The Goddess continued to answer that call...

Chapter 8

Taking this newfound level of perception from technique to artistry was my next goal. I think that at this point, I remember laughing about the fact that one hundred and fifty years earlier, this may have qualified me for a stake burning. Reality just became stranger as we applied the concept of deepening and expanding the connection to neutral space-holding.

I won't get into too much detail, but in the Craniosacral specialization, I not only was doing partner work (two practitioners hold space for a third person), but we also did the technique to trees in a park, unwinding their roots or trauma caused by excessive and irreverent Parks and Rec. pruning. It wasn't tree hugging, it was tree healing!

If you really listened, you could feel/visualize where the roots were obstructed by man-made civil engineering (pipes, etc.), and even get a sense for the personality of the tree. This sounds *really* crazy, but no more so than you "knowing" what your dog or cat is feeling or thinking (ahem).

If you still don't think it's possible, read a book called The Secret Life of Plants by Peter Tompkins and Christopher Bird. I always direct the huffiest of "moral" vegetarians to this groundbreaking work when my hippie-purist colleagues ride me for continuing to eat meat.

We even did Craniosacral on skeletons! We all didn't know what to make of it at first, but D.M. explained that unreleased tension existed in an energetic state even long after the Soul had left a form. You could call it electro-magnetic karma. I held the ankle-bones of a skeleton laying on one of the tables, and *felt the effing thing rocking in my hands as though CSF were flowing through the pinned-together vertebrae*! This was freaky, but my mind explained it away as though it were an ocean-sound in a seashell.

I almost lost it right there, and had to take a long break outside after I had this experience. So did half of my class. Okay...so, we can heal dead people or something? Well, D.M. would likely say that, 'We heal nothing, but can hold space (or field of awareness) where wholeness can re-exist; I'm only expanding your mind and sense of what's possible.'

I missed our class' fieldtrip to BodyWorlds, where taxidermied human corpses in various phases of systemic exposure are posed in everyday postures and social scenarios for view. I'll bet it was *stupendously* trippy, though. Frozen, posing, fleshless bodies whispering, "Hey Mack, you think you could release this shoulder blade, man? I've been holding this handstand for an age, brother."

How could we do that without touching them physically, you may rightly ask?

Well, in Level Four we progressed to doing distance work (like in Reiki II). Our partner would stand in front of us, and gazing neutrally at them, holding space, information about their tensions in their bodies would visually arrive to my mind as though I were in miniature and standing inside of them, observing everything.

Or, their whole body would kind of blur into an outline, leaving only the system or organ that had an issue. As I observed those pictures and diagrams, they would release tension (confirmed by the partner and D.M. herself).

Sometimes the focus would be drawn away from the physical body and into the space around it. When whatever drew my attention shifted, I could also feel a corresponding change in the physical (softening tissue, blood flow, deeper and effortless respiration, etc.) This demonstrated to me on a very deep level how the energy that surrounds our body can and does affect our health, and our consciousness habits.

I've witnessed classmates and clients alike breakdown into tears after a simple shift of energy in one of the layers of their aura. For an hour or more. It sounds like bullshit on the surface, but when you've seen the depth and reach of its effects hundreds of times, you shed your doubt, go with it, and trust something real is happening.

As my father once wisely said, 'The proof is in the puddin', boy."

Side story: My dad is the greatest barometer for bullshit on Earth that I've ever encountered. He's a self-described Darwinist in the classical sense: If you could prove it was real or demonstrate it for his eyes, he would believe it then. For the last ten years I've shared every crazy-sounding thing that I've discovered with him, and he's been compassionate enough to merely raise his eyebrows and politely listen to my ravings.

I tell him everything because he's the least judgmental person I've met (especially where I'm concerned). So he surprised the hell out of me when he challenged me to fix his "messed-up" shoulder.

I really wanted to show my hero that I wasn't wasting my life learning this stuff, so I was excited and terrified to work on this born skeptic, my first big test. At this time, my dad was unable to lift his arm at certain angles and heights without pain, and fifteen twitchy minutes later, he moved it through a pain-free and completely open range of motion.

He looked completely stunned. He looked up at me with a now-wary smile and finally said, 'I guess you weren't bullshitting, son, you really can heal people with your energy stuff.'

'Does the puddin' got proof, Pop?'

'Yep. Yeah, I'd have to say that it does.'

Second biggest skeptic: My cousin and gifted attorney, Paul Rodriguez (not the comic). I told him this story a few years back and he didn't hesitate, with all love, to deem it madness. Until Dad backed me up. Jack Ramay's word is gold and Law.

Paul's inner-skeptic conflicted with this substantial endorsement, but he had injured his shoulder while exercising and it had bothered him for months. He's still a little freaked-out to this day that in 20 minutes of twitching and unwinding, his shoulder condition had disappeared and has not returned. He's a faithful Christian in the traditional sense, and "people aren't supposed to be able to do that," but he'll still admit that it happened.

The two greatest skeptics I know personally validated the strangest therapeutic techniques (philosophically) that I had learned to date. Sweet.

The most trusting man I've ever known and probably the biggest-hearted, is my brotha' from anotha' motha', Sonny Croudo.

When we met, he was the owner and operator of a restaurant right next door to the massage clinic I worked at. He was born and raised in Mexico City and is old enough to be my father. Sonny has two daughters of his own, whom he raised on his own for many years after his wife passed, and they are amazing young women.

We seemed to be the best of friends from our very first conversation. Sometimes, or often, I can tell instantly about someone when I meet them, look in their eyes and shake their hand. Sonny is so rare because he has no guile, or intent to harm, in him. I knew that here stood a man with a deep capacity to Love and completely worthy of trust. Kindness is one of his magical masteries. I think to this day that seekers take self-help seminars to become who he is in character naturally.

Anyway, one day I was on a break in between massage clients, and we were smoking on his restaurant patio: His business had been stagnating and he looked worried. I told him that he should visualize a line going out of his door and the tables packed with happy, sticky-fingered customers (he owned an amazing barbeque joint).

Being positive, and seeing only what you wish to see occur were fundamental to the Law of Attraction, I mention. Your mind electromagnetically attracts or "creates" your reality, as portrayed in the movies <u>What the Bleep Do We Know?!</u>, or <u>The Secret</u> (the movie, *not the book*, that features Esther Hicks/Abraham in it. Don't bother with the new version without Esther, or the book version).

Sonny looked a little confused, but promised to try.

After my long shift, I cruised back over to the restaurant and he held his arms wide, beaming at me. 'My friend, my friend! It worked like magic! I had a record day! TELL ME MORE! TELL ME EVERYTHING!'

So I did. We started with the Law of Attraction and how the mind creates reality through thought. Sonny's eyes kept widening as I explained the basic tenets of its theory and application as explained in the book <u>Ask and It Is Given: How to Manifest Your Dreams In This Lifetime</u> by Esther and Jerry Hicks.

In my small opinion, after having explored what was available to us, I've found it to be the greatest and best work on this subject. A close second would be the works of Wallace Wattles, whose work inspired the creation of the movie <u>The Secret</u>. Suffice it to say that if these are not in your personal library, then they should be. I would have done **anything** to know this stuff growing up, but schools don't teach this stuff yet;-).

Sonny wasn't even phased when I told him the information was channeled by an entity/master named Abraham. 'My cousin Becky in Mexico channels a Master for clients too. I've seen it before and she's amazing,' he said smiling.

Nice. Major obstacle of doubt number one cleared... check!

I mentioned that there's a movie that was made to demonstrate how it all worked called <u>The Secret</u> and that Esther Hicks is channeling Abraham as a featured presenter in it. He almost pleaded to watch it and even asked to bring his daughters with him. Smart dad.

We watched the film at my place and they had lots of questions, but understood every concept perfectly. Since this day, both girls have acquired an amazing ability to manifest whatever they want, but none more so than Nesly's journey with personal healing: Where the Law of Attraction's theorems demand satisfaction and results because someone is in discomfort or pain.

There's a chapter in the movie where a gentleman who survived a plane crash and horrific injuries heals himself through these principles and walks out of the hospital after being *paralyzed*.

Then *his wife* describes how through positive thinking and thanking God for her healing (in advance of its appearance!), she actually healed an enormous tumor in her breast. The before-and-after x-rays were the most telling.

Sonny touched the screen, and looking back at his youngest daughter, says 'See, Nes. We need to practice this together so we all get real good at it.'

When Nesly was a newborn, there was a viral outbreak of sepsis in her hospital nursery. She lost both heads of her femurs so her legs moved uncomfortably in the sockets, and bone tissue in her shoulders had dissolved.

As her body matured, an extreme case of scoliosis developed that doctors were sure would require corrective surgery. Nesly had been bravely wearing a corrective brace around her torso to help with the condition.

Can you imagine what this was like for a 13-year-old girl in this culture?

She had every right to complain, and never has.

I still had to do a ten-session project with the same client to complete my Craniosacral Specialization, so we could really witness the power of progressive treatments. When I inquired whether Nesly would like to be my subject or not, Sonny agreed immediately and wanted to begin the sessions right then.

For Nesly, it was a chance to embrace an alternative reality previously not thought possible. D.M. explained that there had been case studies at the Upledger Institute where through consistent treatments, clients experienced the impossible: Bone re-growth and even the healing of spinal chord injuries. I'm talking about folks told they'll be in a wheelchair for life becoming mobile again.

The greatest healer in the world, in my esteem, is Jon of God in Brazil. He has facilitated this miracle for many over the decades and specializes in the impossible, but I was and am still a novice next to this Giant in Spirit. I'll write about Jon later, though.

I was personally excited by the project because I'd never done more than two sessions with the same person, and Nesly's spinal curvature was like a game of Janga that had been played for half an hour. The results would be highly noticeable, or should be. We both couldn't wait to begin.

From our first session to our tenth, extraordinary changes occurred. If I possessed a shred of doubt left about the efficacy of energy work, it fled from me when our project had concluded.

I won't bore you with too many hallelujah(!) details, but her spinal curvature had been deviating from its midline 1 degree every month, like a drifting tectonic plate. After our appointments, **it had corrected 11° back *toward the midline*.**

Her deviation not only halted, it came back eleven freaking degrees! When her spinal specialist took x-rays of Nesly to evaluate her for a future surgery, Sonny told me (while laughing his ass off) how the doctor's face looked when he was mining for a sane explanation as to why her spine had moved.

Sonny explained the treatments she had been receiving from me, and the doc didn't know what to make of it, but both agreed to give Nesly more time to grow and mature, reviewing her options for surgery later.

My Craniosacral class cheered when I retold that part, because altering our country's medical paradigm toward preventative philosophy and provoking idiopathic responses is one of our highest thoughts for tomorrow's healing arts.

We were just beginning to witness the fringe of how miraculous and wondrous life could be, and would become for me as well.

I achieved my "specialist" certification in Craniosacral Therapy and, of course, immediately turned my attention to becoming a Reiki Master Teacher. Jeannie was offering a two-day Level 3 course at her home in the desert an hour away.

I wanted to go so bad, but it cost $350 that I didn't have. I wasn't complaining, because at one point in the Reiki system's evolution it cost as much as $10,000 to receive the Master attunement. $350 was a steal.

It never ceases to amaze me how effective the feeling and experience of lack can be for Divinity to get our attention at times. I prayed until my brain and chest throbbed. I had a feeling that the Universe received my request.

I know now that Spirit responds with greater depth when you thank *in advance of a prayer's manifestation*, instead of supplication, but I know it sounded like, 'Please please please please pleeeeease!' Perhaps like any child, I hoped that I could annoy my Father into giving-in.

Usually, this prayer method to the Universe is not met with success. It did this time, though, because it was time for me. A friend floated me the money I lacked to take the class, and I called Jeannie as fast as I could to enroll. It felt right on every level of my being, and I felt ready for the next level of experience.

Usually, the next step would find me, and introduce itself in an unexpected or uncomfortable manner, but I had been flowing with Reiki every day and every way I could since the second attunement. I couldn't wait to feel the upgrade in energy and have the ability to pass it on to others: That deeper, encompassing buzz of connecting with Divine energies.

The first day of instruction and attunements were sacred, wonderful, and powerful beyond my expectations. I just felt like a tube of light most of the time. Learning the metaphysical applications of Reiki to life as a complete spiritual path or as an enhancement to one's religion was inspiring.

If you studied and utilized the Usui Reiki system only as your way of consciously evolving, I am confident that it would carry you to the finish line of whatever spiritual goal you desired. It's a wonderful, complete system.

I loved learning and giving the attunement ceremonies. You have to learn the protocols and steps for all three levels, obviously, but when you actually attune someone, a *crazy* amount of energy comes through (at least that's what I've always experienced, almost intoxicated on energy).

I remember the sensation of floating for a week after the class, and waves of tingling and heat after giving my tenth attunement (I was slightly obsessed with getting it correct and got carried away...especially out of my mind). I was almost spinning as I lay in bed that night, my arms and hands pulsing incessantly with my now higher Reiki-wattage.

I always love the part of the process where my physical body acclimates to new or greater energy flows, the sensations of blockages melting and neurons surging with information; an expanding heart-space allowing greater Light and Life.

The second day was just as magical as the first, with more meditation, organic meals, laughter, tears, and expansion. I felt ready to attune the world, to share the vast gifts I had received with everyone.

During a meditation, I had a wonderful vision of going to elementary and middle schools, speaking with open-minded parents about the potential benefits of their children practicing and mastering Reiki during Open Houses. I saw myself at hospital nurseries, attuning babies in the ICU to the 2nd level to ease their healing processes (I was one of them. I wouldn't attune them to Master level because that should be a consciously elected choice, though I'd gladly do so for any consenting parent).

I saw too many wonderful potential happenings for our culture's futures to share them here, but if even half of them happen, then you'll see a world others have proclaimed impossible for at least another couple of generations. Perhaps in another book at another time.

After integrating the experience by soaking in a Soul-nurturing mineral/sulfur springs pool nearby for a few hours, I was ready to go back to The Big Dirty, or societal humanity as it is currently embraced.

I always feel at least a pang of sorrow when leaving the pristine spiritual environments and energies that these trips and classes offer me. Many of my spiritual friends and affiliates live in these places all of the time; a big city's general collective consciousness and noise is too toxic for their comfort, and dampens their ability to live a life focused on the Divine.

In another way, I'm really grateful that I don't *have* to live this way. The frontlines of The War for humanity's heart and mind are in the marketplace anyway, not a cave or ashram. The buggle world doesn't annoy me so much.

It's totally rigged for awful, but it's salvageable! We'll make it happen!

When I returned to San Diego, I resumed my searching and researching of the ascensionary, or spiritually evolving process. I came across a book called <u>A Little Light on</u>

Ascension by Diana Cooper. This angelic woman channels an ascended (5D) master by the name of Kumeka, and has lovingly simplified for her readers how the process works, citing many of the Masters, Elohim, and Archangels I'd heard of (and a few I hadn't). Learning about their particular specialties within service to God's creation, and the 50 Golden Keys to ascension at its conclusion, make purchasing this book highly worth it.

The greatest gem I mined from this resource was finding another ascension author she cited named Dr. Joshua David Stone. She writes that in his book, The Complete Ascension Manual: How to Achieve Ascension in This Lifetime, Dr. Stone describes an energy now available to the Earth and humanity called The Mahatma, or Avatar of Synthesis. Also, that when invoked (prayed to) would accelerate one's evolution by one thousand times.

Whaaaaaat?! *Did that lady say 'By one thousand fold?!'*

Where did I put my freaking Barnes and Nobles card?! Where are my freaking car keys?! Aaaaaaaaaghhh!!!!

Chapter 9

After devouring Dr. Stone's masterpiece, the first emotion I felt (after days of awe) was incredible relief. I thought I would be pouring all of my life's energies into extracting from these sacred texts the most useful information I could, and synthesizing for folks how they are interrelated. I bless Dr. Stone daily for accomplishing this vast task for me.

He not only makes plain the sources I had come across, but also discovered highly powerful techniques from many I hadn't. From barely understandable texts like <u>The Urantia Book</u>, <u>The Book of Knowledge: The Keys of Enoch</u>, and Helena Blavatski's <u>The Secret Doctrine</u>, to the works of Alice Bailey and Janet McClure, Dr. Stone has put together the most comprehensive encyclopedia of evolutionary knowledge I have come across to this day.

Much like the Mahatma, he's synthesized everything. Every obscure insight I'd had, this fellow had validated or taken further. It's amazing.

Now, what I'm about to express may not make much sense (or any), and probably qualifies me for pharmaceutical prescriptions, but bear with me.

If you ask your more informed and researched New-Agey-New-Ager, he or she may have referenced important dates in humanity's and Earth's recent history. Two universally discussed events occurred or will occur in 1987 and 2012.

That second number look familiar? Ever wonder what the hell it was all about? We'll get there. First things first, and why it's important to our spiritual evolution.

According to Dr. Stone, Janet McClure, Serapis, and about one hundred other mystics who channel masters or entities, in 1987 humanity and Earth reached a zenith in our growth and experience together. This event was called the Harmonic Convergence.

To experience this game of Karma and separation from our Source, we had to collectively decide as a species to shut down our conscious connection to Oneness and Now-ness to enjoy the glory of reconnecting with it all eventually.

Like Spiritual amnesia, or Cosmic hide-and-seek (that we play with our Soul). Reconnecting consciously with our Divine origins ends the game. The Harmonic Convergence was the end to our 3D virtual reality foray here.

The Mahatma, or Avatar of Synthesis (Biblically: The Rider on the Pale Horse), is the aspect of God or Source that connects every other dimension, system, species, etc. in Infinite Creation. Like the connective tissue in our body that surrounds everything in it.

This Being of Collective Consciousness encompasses every level of evolution throughout all planes of Source's being, calling everything back unto Itself once everything has been explored. In our and Earth's creative game (yes, Gaia is an evolving, living entity whom volunteered as our "game board") the twist we devised for ourselves was duality (polarity), karma, or *what would happen if we could choose against God's perfect will **in every possible way**.*

Look at our world today. Did we do a great job or what?

Well, buddy, good news. We're on our way home to Papa.

Scientists today are befuddled (I love that word!) as to the reasons why the Earth's measurable physical energy itself is rising at an unprecedented and apparently exponential rate. Solar flares, ditto. As the planet is releasing the toxicity (humanity's misused energy from Source), She's supposedly gonna shake, quake, move, stretch, and sweat (volcanic eruptions, extreme weather, floods, pole shifts, earthquakes, etc.) just like we would during an intense energy treatment: Just correspondingly huger, as Dumbledore would say.

You may have noticed that up until this point, I've refrained from utilizing too many Jerry Potter references.

Well, time-in bitches! Time to kick the weirdness meter up another notch!

Yes, by the way, I am a Potter nerd. You may have gleaned that from the title.

As a nerd growing up, I realized that I had no "cool" nerd obsession like the other geeks. No D&D, Star Wars, Star Trek (though I'm now a lay-Trekie), or Lord of the Rings. No comics, Japanese animae, or conventions attended thereof. Can't speak Klingon a lick.

Then my father (who's probably read 4,000 books) raved to me about the Sherry Potter books.

'Children's books?' I asked.

'Literature,' he replied grinning.

I am moderately embarrassed to admit that I've read the entire seven-book series at least ten times, and could possibly teach a university-level survey course in Philosophy using the material from these novels alone. Solomon Rushdie, I hear, is a huge Potter fan also, so it's okay. I pray that we'll develop a curriculum together and geek-out over the physics of J.K. Rowling's parallel universe one day. I even own a Gryffindor sweatshirt (yes, I'm in my 30's and I still rock that shit in public!).

The only thing I take exception to in the Potter series, is that a "Buggle" is a term used to describe *a human who is incapable of magic,* and those who could attend or have attended Bogwarts are the only ones with this capacity. **I say not so.**

To me, a Buggle is an unconscious wizard awaiting his or her awakening to the magic of the Soul. We all have one of those, so essentially, *we're all wizards.*

Please also consider that the origin of the word wizard is "one who is wise" – a wise-ard.

A sorcerer...one who is co-creating with the Source, or God.

Prayer = magic.

Your acceptance letter to this Cosmic School is always forthcoming; it's merely a matter of recognizing that matter is energy, and accepting this new paradigm or world as *real.* Then you gain entrée.

It's like when humanity was digesting that the world is a sphere, and not flat. Or when Germ Theory changed medicine. Then the fun and endless new possibilities abound.

Now, back to the Earth Herself going through the process of ascension. After this Mahatma anchored It's energy (hypothetically, of course), Gaia has been accelerating toward 5th dimensionality *with or without us.* That Golden Earth that I witnessed, but couldn't visit, is apparently the inevitable destination for Her and us. The only snafu is that every cultural system we've created contrary to the Divine Will is probably going to go into an exponential state of dissolution, as the incoming energies no longer support the game of iniquity and separation. Uh-oh.

Will this look like utter chaos to anyone deeply attached to, or immersed in our systems of global politics, military/industrial complexes, medicine (I use the term loosely), economics, commodities, or religion? You bet your sweet ass.

Well, Buddha warned us all about attachment-to-suffering ratios. The end of the world? Only as we know it today...and thank Shiva! Talk about a fixer-upper across the board!

Oh, and depending upon whether you're focusing upon living in the emerging world of Light, Love, and Oneness, or if you're gonna get pulled into the myriad swirling shit-storms that will be these systemic meltdowns, will have to do with what you give your attention and energy to.

There's zero judgment to this process, by the way. Some Souls are going to choose chaos because it serves to balance their remaining karma, and will free them up to evolve somewhere else at a different pace. Others will embrace their divinity, embodied on levels that haven't been seen on this planet ever, or so the theory Jesus laid-out for us stands (...these and greater things you shall do as I return unto my Father...or something like that).

Every Son and Daughter evolves at his or her own pace, kind of like a Montessori school, but there's no judging which path is "better". Everyone graduates (ascends) eventually through embodying many personalities or characters, and all paths lead back to the heart of the Mother/Father God.

To offer this all scope and zesty perspective, I've often asked my clients and students to imagine humanity's 6 billion plus Souls playing a virtual reality, full-immersion video game at the same time, called Planet Earth: Divine Imperfection and Back.

We create and embody thousands of characters, whether bum, king, housewife, murderer, victim, disabled, and so forth until the "avatar" realizes it's the Soul, consciously. Boom! Nirvana and liberation from the wheel of rebirth.

Next level, please Dad.

Now let me ask you something.

When you watch someone playing Grand Theft Auto, or any character-based video game, if the character dies, what do you or that person do? You might be a little disappointed, but you save the game where you left off *and create a new character.* Then you continue. Nothing is lost through the process of what might have been a hundred lives or characters. You can even tailor the looks and characteristics of each character to suit your whim or experiences, right?

Fat, thin, ugly, beautiful, rich, poor, healthy, sickly, according to what you might wish to experience. Sounds a lot like reincarnation, doesn't it?

Do you think your Soul feels any different about the "you" reading this right now? If you don't "get it" during this game, it'll simply save the game and continue at its convenience, with a fresh character where it left off.

You might be thinking, 'Wait, my Soul doesn't care if I croak during this process?!' I'm not *just* saying that, but it may well be seeking a way to die *in the most extreme and creative way possible.* Have you ever become tired of playing because the character couldn't find the way to proceed to the next part of the game, and just kill him/her off in the craziest way just to witness it?

No difference whatsoever.

Don't fret, though. Your Soul wants to win this game far more than we do playing Xbox or PS3, especially because The Great Game is at a culmination point where it's changing

111

into another level of play (at least for Earth). Souls are gonna have to incarnate somewhere else to enjoy the karma-thing, because the new slant, at least for humanity here, will be the first levels of Divine Expression.

The book <u>What is Lightbody?</u> describes the steps of this process of awakening for us and the Earth, even if it's a little non-linear. It's a little weird sounding, and the chronology is a bit off, but there's useful info there, and I'm game. Life here is THE GAME, and the only real one going on. You may as well play, so PLAY YOUR ASS OFF LIKE YOU WANT TO WIN!

What's winning? Being Love while doing whatever your heart desires.

So, as predicted by several indigenous spiritual cultures (Hopi and Mayans to name a few), around the end of the year 2012 (around December 21, 2012) this energetic turnover point is supposed to happen.

The (predicted) semantics involved ranged from the end of our perception of linear time (Nowness' return), or perhaps a collective enlightenment experience and awareness of our Oneness (spontaneous 5th dimensionality and a physics relationship change between how long it takes for us to think something and its manifestation in our experience). Also, the possibility of alien cousins dropping-in Star Trek-style (First Contact). Very exciting hypothesis' all.

A few people are pretty sure the Earth will end, or that humanity will end itself in a total meltdown, fighting over resources. These are invariably the same folks who were barking the same crap during Y2K. Good call, ref. Good call.

Feeling good is your guide to intuitively correct choosing, and is a choice of and in itself, as Abraham/Hicks would say. Choosing to anticipate something wonderful for everyone in

2012 seems the wisest course for me, and I invite you to join me in humanity's wake-up resurrection party.

I'm always on the lookout for those who're prolifically inviting everyone to join this expanding Oneness-fest, even if they don a peculiar appearance and kooky, New-Agey-sounding names.

Actually, *especially* if they have the courage to do so in today's passively judgmental Self-Help scene (many think that they poop potpourri in this emerging field).

I must admit that even unto this joy-filled day, that no one I have met or studied-with more accurately fits this description than Wisdom Teacher Sri Ram Kaa, and his Beloved twin Soul, the Oracle Kira Raa.

I was amazed to walk into my massage clinic in 2005 and come across a flier advertising an ascension workshop one hour away in Orange County. I was moderately skeptical because I was still a bit prejudiced against the well-to-do at the time, and the O.C. is a fairly affluent area (as seen and stereotyped on television).

However, I was fiending for expansion at the time, and the couple on the flier couldn't have looked the part more if they'd tried (flowing Indian-style garb, bindi on the forehead). As I was irresistibly attracted to the strange and unusual (nothing *usual* or *conventional* ever possessing anything remotely powerful for me), of course I went.

When I arrived, I immediately noticed that everyone had deep, perceptive eyes, and I was the youngest there by ten years at least. These folks all had the air of being seasoned seekers (not a wizards' sporting term). When everyone was settled in our host's beautiful living room, the couple took their places in the chairs set out for them in front of us. I felt my breath catch in my chest as they lovingly surveyed us all.

Sri Ram Kaa was a larger version of Dumbledore. As he smiled at the crowd, I followed his intense blue eyes flickering everywhere, taking-in the energy of the room. He wore an all-white one-piece like the gurus in India or Egypt might wear, and he even had long white hair and a short-trimmed beard. He looked larger than life and filled with energy.

Kira Raa, his wife, felt like and appeared as a divine manifestation of the Goddess and Mother, but when she spoke, you could feel the strength and authority in her voice (while not channeling). She was bedecked with crystal necklaces, her trademark bindi over her third eye, and beautifully ornate Indian-style clothing. She had long, dark hair and even deeper eyes that I'm sure could see only precious Souls. Kira seemed to embody every face of the Goddess I had researched, from Parvarti to Durga, and Athena. Wow, was all I could think.

Sri and Kira took one another's hands, and then took out a pair of hand-sized cylindrical objects; one that was silver, and one that looked copper-ish. Sri put the silver one in his available hand and Kira did the same with the other. Then I felt the energy of the room increase (heat, buzzing) as they closed their eyes and began making "bliss faces."

Have you ever seen Woody Allen in "Sleeper" when he's pretending to be an android in the future, and there's a metallic ball getting passed around a party that gets the holder intoxicated, and he hilariously keeps snatching it back? It looked like that.

What the heck are those? I wondered. Yet before asking someone next to me who also had an inquisitive expression, Sri Ram Kaa began to welcome us and offer his wisdom discourse.

I'll admit now, that I'd never heard a metaphysical teaching or description of Universal Law in such a succinct, penetrating, and simplified presentation. I was floored, even as I was sitting upon one. I suspected his spiritual background and training to be as extensive as anyone I'd encountered or more so, but the basis of his darshan (teaching) was from the multidimensional offerings his wife had received the previous few years.

I was deeply impressed (not an easy thing to do at this point) and he held my rapt attention.

He laughingly described during one of Kira's insoulments (total embodiment channeling) of the Archangel Zadkiel, how he had pleaded for a word or mantra to share with humanity to deepen its connection to the divine process of ascension.

Abashed, he said, the Archangelic Presence replied (and with their permission):

I AM HERE! ('I...I know' he replied).
I AM READY! (Oh.)
I AM OPEN! (Uh-huh).
GUIDE ME!©

'That is all, Sri Ram Kaa,' spoke the lips of his wife's body.

We all laughed really hard at that, and he shook like a younger, fitter Santa Claus. Then Kira took her turn to speak.

She explained that she had physically, medically died twice (not on purpose) to prepare her body to house this and other Divine consciousnesses for this level of channeling. That when she invited in Zadkiel, her soul would retreat into her Beloved's body who held a spiritual space for her, and her vacated form could be completely animated by Him, remembering nothing of what happened when it was concluded.

Okaaaaaay, spoke the receding part of my mind still susceptible to doubt. This was a new one.

She shifted in her chair and smoothed her dress to be more comfortable and a hush went throughout the room. As Sri Ram Kaa placed an arm around her shoulders, she closed her eyes, took a deep breath, and collapsed in her chair like a marionette.

Everyone tried to stifle a gasp as three seconds later her head and torso popped back up, eyes wide and alight with energy and exclaimed, 'Hello!' in a different toned, Eastern European accent (I think). Then the energy in the room increased ten-fold and my spine began to throb.

WTF! I remember thinking, even though I was barely capable of thought at all. Are you kidding me?

For a half-hour, this presence who announced itself as the Archangel Zadkiel, gave a synopsis of the path of "Self-Ascension™," the mantra offered to Sri Ram Kaa, and the coming Earth-changes leading up to the year 2012. Then He directly fielded and answered personal questions from the guests in attendance. The messages were blowing the questioners, and therefore me, away. Unfreaking-believably accurate answers to highly personalized and specific inquiries. My doubt was ebbing from me, but I was still in shock.

When Zadkiel thanked us and left her body, Kira was still in a kind of trance, but was giving each of us a hug and Shaktiput (a type of spiritual blessing referenced in Hinduism). I won't repeat here what she whispered in my ear when Sri Ram Kaa steered her body in my direction, but I can say I had never felt Love of that quality and force in my life and the top of my head was Mt. Vesuvius. Allahu Akbar! Sai Ram! Shalom *and* mazal tov!

After the workshop had concluded, many of us milled around, making small talk about our backgrounds and exclaiming our amazement at what we had witnessed. One lady I spoke to introduced herself as Michele, and we found an immediate connection through Reiki. She was a Master/ Teacher as well and had apparently put on many successful classes in the local area. She also did about thirty other spiritual services, including past-life regressions (cool).

Eyes swimming with tears, Michele says that she was my mother during a lifetime we shared in Atlantis as part of its highest priesthood. I gave her a hug, thinking, sure, why not? She had a familiar and mothering energy. For all I knew, she had been.

Then she tells me about a new kind of Reiki that was an addendum to the Usui system that was new and rare, and she had just finished her Master/Teacher level of training in it.

Oh boy, I thought, here we go again. Another "new" Reiki system being channeled so someone out there can hop up and down, going, 'I channeled a new Reiki system only I can pass on and (of course) trademark.' There's about one hundred of these "new" systems that were supposed to be the end-all.

Almost reading my mind, Michele says, 'I know what you're thinking, but this is different. It's *by far* the most powerful thing I've come across to date. It was the Atlantean system that was used for healing and spiritual evolution (WTF, I think. Atlantean?). Saint Germain re-established it in 1996 and there are 352 symbols.'

'Wait,' I said, 'WTF did you just say? Did you just say 352 symbols?! *The Mahatma!?!*'

Her jaw dropped. '*You know about the Mahatma energy?!*' she asks, eyes popping. 'You're further along than I thought at your age. I'm a little jealous. Actually, Shamballa Reiki, or Shamballa Multidimensional Healing is a combination of the Mahatma, the 12th Ray (Christ Consciousness), and the collective consciousness of all of the Ascended Masters and Lady Masters.'

I almost fainted and wanted to throw-up, but did neither. I probably just looked dumb with my mouth hanging open, then pathetic as I began begging her to teach me. With a sympathetic smile, she agreed, saying that that was how she looked to her friend when *she* found out about it. She wasn't going to charge me a thing for the classes, either.

'We are family after all,' she dry-sobbed, as we embraced again.

I almost cried too. I thought I was walking a few inches off of the floor as I found my way to my car.

Two weeks later, I arranged an informal class with Michele at her house for my Shamballa Level 1 attunement. I discovered that she offered practical and spiritual guidance for many people, not only for clients, in her local area and served at The Goddess Temple in Orange County. I was doubly grateful that she was going to teach and guide me on her own time and dime.

She began with a meditation (of course) and explained the system's ancient and recent (albeit mythological) history. As the story is presented, St. Germain (an Ascended Master with whom I'm very familiar with) had a previous incarnation (lifetime) as the High Priest of Atlantis who, before the deluge (as depicted in the Torah) had foreseen the society's impending destruction and moved his operation to the Tibet area.

Hoping to reestablish the priesthood there, he leaked a few of the Shamballa symbols to the local residents (the four recently rediscovered Usui Reiki symbols) to see if they were spiritually mature enough to not misuse their power. They were not. The system did not at that time have the safety precautions and boundaries that render the powerful energy harmless, as today.

To this day, a few of the ancient monasteries in Tibet display these Usui Reiki symbols on their walls.

After his ascension following the French Revolution, this Comte de St. Germaine waited until 1996 to reestablish the full spectrum of this system via the Mahatma (Great Father) and a spiritual teacher from Scotland named John Armitage (aka Hari Das Melchizedek). Not many folks even within the Reiki community have ever heard of it, but my habit of asking for the most powerful and highest systems seemed to have prevailed again (crazy origin story notwithstanding).

I asked Michele if I'd have to learn to draw and memorize all 352 symbols (each one accessing another level of initiation in the Mother/Father's creation), and she said no with a chuckle. There were four levels to the system, and only twenty-two consciously known symbols, so I was inwardly relieved. Also, that by Level 3 I'd have the ability to attune others to the energy. Level 4 meant I could attune Master/Teachers.

If I had a bit, I'd have been chomping at it vigorously.

Level One had super-charged all of the symbols I'd already been utilizing (Usui Reiki), and there were discourses by several Masters in the manual that Michele had printed-out for me.

I'd never felt this connected to Source, so powerfully flowing was the energy coursing through me. So much so that once I did a hands-on energy session upon returning, and I left deep red handprints upon the client's back. Sometimes I felt like I could cook a chicken with my bare hands.

Michele said that we should wait three weeks in-between each level to allow for emotional and physical integration, so I reluctantly agreed. I could barely contain my desire for more, but could understand the wisdom of waiting. All great things come to those who can chill, or something to that effect.

After my insanely powerful Level 3 class, I found out that Sri Ram Kaa and Kira Raa were planning a spiritual trip and had been given a directive by the Archangelic realm to go to Peru to anchor an ascension portal, and hold many ceremonies with different local shaman for over a week and a half. Also that twenty-nine people were invited to join them to assist with the process.

I began my pleading with the Universe, only to discover the trip was filled already.

Bugger.

Pinche mierda, I exclaimed.

Then by some vast miracle, I manifested a friend of mine with ascensionary leanings who had the capacity to cover the costs if only two spaces were to open up.

My vibration began to match that of an eight-year-old strolling the aisles of a Toys-R-Us one week before Christmas. At the same time, a newly cultivated attitude of, 'Well, if it's meant to be, it'll happen,' began to flicker through my mind during intensely prolonged sessions of longing.

Less than a month before the trip, two spaces were vacated.

I was going to get to see Machu Picchu!

Thank you Mother, Father, Allah, Yahweh, Buddha, Brahman, Brahwoman, Dattatreya, and everyone else I forgot to thank. I don't *care* that the orchestra is playing or that the red light is flashing! I did it! Whoooo hooooo! (My apologies, Cuba).

One tiny problem, though. I was still smoking a pack a day, and most of the trip involved hiking at about a 10,000-foot altitude. I had visions of clutching my ribcage and begging people twice my age to wait-up for me.

I thought I was screwed.

As Hermione would do, were she in my shoes, I retreated to one of my favorite places: The New Age section of the local Barnes and Noble, to gather my thoughts and such (libraries not typically containing the info I'm Spiritually interested in). I remember gazing at the ceiling, having failed to quit cigarettes several times in the past and feeling rather miserable about it, when my eyes involuntarily glanced downward.

An insulting title stared back at me.

The Easyway to Quit Smoking Cigarettes by Allen Carr.

I started laughing out-loud where I stood.

Easy?! What jerk wrote this tripe? I wondered, my ego stinging. Easy?!!

I couldn't wait to read this guy's B.S. technique before scoffing and tossing it on my mind's compost heap.

Hmmm, I thought, flipping through its pages. He claims that over 90% of the folks that come to his clinics worldwide successfully leave non-smokers. That he held no degrees, only that he'd failed at every technique possible, and his expertise stemmed from breaking *an 80-100 cigarette-a-day chain-smoking pattern for over 30 years*. That he'd stumbled onto the solution by accident.

That resonated with me a little, and he wrote the book in the same manner as I'm attempting to communicate here. Like he was talking to you, not at you or down to you. Plus, the dude was funny. I kept reading for a while, but I had to put it down, because it made me want to smoke from just thinking about it so much.

After sucking one down outside the store (I live in California after all), I couldn't believe that I couldn't argue one point the guy was making.

Are you kidding me? This is your answer to my prayer? I asked, as I began to tingle all over.

If I'd only known.

His methods were simple. Keep smoking the whole time you read the book, and there will come a time at the end, after you hear what he has to say, where you'll smoke your last cigarette *and* it will be easy.

'Yeah effing right,' grumbled my ego, and the nicotine in my vascular system.

Mr. Carr pin-points the problem as **the nicotine** and the subtle psychological nuances the drug and the ego utilize to get you to light that next cigarette. Then, he rips to shreds more efficiently than Johnny Cochran, every myth associated with the presumed benefits of smoking.

Utterly, and completely to shreds.

After this, Mr. Carr enumerates the incredible benefits of becoming a non-smoker again, which are many. Once you surprisingly discover and realize that you do wish to become one and it won't be an excruciating path, but easy, you only have to do two things; two simple things to remember as the nicotine clears your system over three weeks:

1. Every time the nicotine nibbles at you, begging you to light one up or buy a pack, you exclaim to yourself, 'Thank God I'm a non-smoker!' and mentally review all of the wonderful benefits you'll be shortly reclaiming (substitute Brahma, Buddha, Allah, YHVH, or whatever reference you have in connection with the All). And...

2. Remember with gratitude the mantra, *'There's no such thing as just one cigarette,'* which would put you right back into being an addict again, and another three weeks.

Unflippingbelievably simple. Re-framing *who you are* using a positive, instead of thinking that you're "giving-up" something in the negative. As Allan says, you're escaping a trap, and one that will have you for life. If you could even call that a Life.

I can say with all honestly that this is one of the three most important, most valuable books I've read in my entire life.

I feel as though Mr. Carr has given me at least the possibility of living 30 years longer, with greater quality, and not only may have eventually saved it, but also about 100,000 future dollars that would have otherwise gone to death-merchants. I feel I owe him a debt of gratitude that I am incapable of reciprocating, or even expressing here.

May he and his family be blessed by the Universe in the Highest, and in all ways. I'm writing this with my eyes filled with tears.

If someone you love smokes cigarettes and is struggling to quit, buy them this magical book.

You may just save their life.

Chapter 10

So, having reclaimed my identity (and energy) as a non-smoker, I readied myself with preparations to travel to Peru. The itinerary for the trip sounded sensational, and the accommodations just as outstanding.

Our group would be led by a well-respected shaman, or holy man, and the tour company organizing the trip had us lodging at four and five-star hotels the entire trip. Roughing-it didn't seem to resonate with these pilgrims, and I sure as *hell* wasn't complaining.

The reasoning for which was that we would have so many intensely transformative spiritual experiences and ceremonies, that it would be prudent to not integrate the (sometimes) uncomfortable changes in uncomfortable surroundings. Made sense to me! Although I had to admit, having never traveled outside of the U.S., I was a tad apprehensive about the rating systems for hotels and if it were a sliding-scale, relative to other nations' standards (I know, I know).

My concerns were allayed the moment I left the plane. A warmly smiling, blue-suited local greeted my friend and I, and led us to our tour bus after loading our luggage on a trolley. When I say *our* tour bus, I mean that he came to the airport in the most luscious bus with televisions I'd ever rode upon. Just to pick *us* up and take us to the nicest hotel in Lima where our traveling companions were staying.

I knew then that this would be the trip of a lifetime.

Our driver explained, as we rolled through the endless urban sprawl that was Peru's largest city, that it was home to over 8 million people. All were trying to scrape a living or carve-out a piece of empire; where Mercedes dealerships shared a city block space with condemned buildings, their roof-tops lined with upturned, broken glass bottles to keep thieves or intruders away.

The duality of modern Westernization's influence was displayed in sharp relief before our very eyes.

Our guide mentioned that he himself was raised in Cuzco, the former inland spiritual epicenter of the Incan Empire where we'd take a small airplane to the following day. I wasn't exactly thrilled by this prospect, having watched La Bamba about ten times, but I felt divinely guided. I was praying far more often for the safe arrival of my suitcase, to be honest.

After an incredible lunch at the hotel and settling-in, I finally met Sri Ram Kaa and Kira Raa in the lobby. They glowed with palpable joy and embraced me as though we were long-lost family. Inviting a few others who greeted them and myself to dinner later, they encouraged us to wander around the local neighborhood and see the amazing shops filled with artisan-craft.

Peru, they said, is famous for its gemstone jewelry and craftsmanship, but they also admonished us to pace ourselves with purchases because we'd have even better opportunities as our journey progressed.

As I was on a fairly tight discretionary budget for extras on the trip, it wasn't that difficult to resist. However, it wasn't hard to imagine being set loose with ten grand to blow, evaporating with relative ease in these storefronts. Beautiful barely describes the artistic offerings that were on display, both with the silver work and semi-precious gemstones. Beautiful.

At dinner, it didn't escape my notice that everyone was insisting on vegetarian cuisine or vegan. Even a couple of the folks were wrinkling their faces when the waiter described a dish with a meat-base. Uh-oh, I thought.

I was raised a meat-and-potatoes boy and hadn't adopted the rabbit-food, non-sentient being diet yet. Perhaps I never would, however I didn't want to give my companions the impression that I was some blood-crazed carnivore (at least not on our first day together...I had a mid-rare filet mignon at the hotel restaurant earlier anyway, so I was cool).

The next day, we were bused back to the Lima airport to fly to Cuzco forty-five minutes away, and I sighed with relief when we were boarding a brand-new, mid-sized airplane. I conversed with the fellow participants in our group and found them all to be energetic and fascinating. The landscape was painted with the snow-capped Andes Mountains and barren surrounding terrain. When we landed smoothly it was at about 11,000 feet above sea level.

In San Diego, I'd go on really long walks and even a few hikes to ready my body for this trip, but nothing prepared me for the molasses-wading and aching fatigue that was simply walking at this altitude. Thankfully, the moment we all arrived, a few grinning locals were instantly upon us all to sell us candies made from the coca leaf: Peru's treasured, and oft misconstrued national wonder-plant.

As we sucked on the candies, we all started to feel a little bit more clear-headed as we trudged toward our deluxe tour bus (which was surprising for so remote-looking a location. Romulo, the owner and coordinator of Peruvian Magical Journeys whom accompanied us every step of the way, was beyond amazing).

The countryside was breathtaking and the power of the Andes flowed everywhere. My excitement grew as we weaved through the hand-made brick homes that dotted the hillside neighborhoods along the main road that led to the heart of Cuzco.

We arrived outside of our first five-star destination (I could get used to this, I thought). The Hotel de Libertador was Cuzco's finest, and it shared a cobble-stoned square with our first tour destination, the Temple of the Sun.

The main lobby was noteworthy, with high windowed ceilings, beautiful artwork, and coca tea stations. We were often encouraged to drink it by Sri, Kira, and Romulo to acclimate to the high altitude (because they said it contains fourteen alkaloids).

Needless to say, its energy rivaled rooibus tea and it tasted delicious.

Porters brought-up our bags and we all explored the beautiful rooms, which we discovered, came with robes and slippers. (I am a robe advocate, by the way. Any self-respecting mystic should adopt them as their uniform). While I did a small dance of Joy in the room with gratitude for this rolling miracle, I realized that I was late for the first leg of our tour, so I hastened to join the group.

A gentleman that I hadn't seen up until this time was explaining extraordinary things about the Temple of the Sun. Not only was it an astrological observatory that priests would use to discern when the rainy season was coming (if their calculations for planting seed were off, countless people would starve), but there was also an alcove inside where about 46 of the Earth's lay lines (meridians) converged at a single spot.

He invited people to stand on this spot with their feet together, and to close their eyes. Within moments they were smiling and weaving in a circle as though being flushed down a toilet. Then he abruptly led us away (before my turn!) to a touristy part of the temple, looking concerned.

The tour became slightly generic as he elucidated information to us from the posted signs and landmarks. I noticed that our group's numbers had dwindled to about half; that Sri and Kira hadn't accompanied us, and I was growing nauseous as we reached the center of the temple. So were quite a few others. I felt dizzy, and like I was going to hurl. An hour later, I tried to rest in my hotel room, sweating profusely, thinking, man, this altitude thing is worse that I'd thought.

When everyone joined for dinner, though, Sri and Kira (and a few other clairvoyants on our trip) gave another story, explaining their absences and early departures.

Spanish conquistadores apparently had slaughtered the hundred or so priests in residence there, and by the looks on their faces, I could tell that the blood had flowed as rivers. My spine crawled in validation, and my blood turned cold.

Despite this gruesome pronouncement, the vibration slowly grew jubilant when a local band sauntered-over for a spirited live performance and (of course) CD's for sale. Musicians are the same the world round, I suppose. We danced and cheered as children do.

That evening, Kira Raa and Sri Ram Kaa ushered us into a conference room for an angelic session with Zadkiel, and to introduce us formally to Don Ruben, our tour's mystery man

("Don" being a title of spiritual respect). Apparently, besides being a fully qualified Quechua "pacco" ('Shaman is a word invented by a white man,' he says), he also held a doctorate in Chemistry and studied with Jesuit priests for over a decade.

He gave an amazing, rare account of the hidden mysteries of the Inca not found in books, and of their spiritual scientific epicenter named "Picchu" (not Machu Picchu...another white guy from Yale) which meant "vortex" in the indigenous tongue.

Ruben had little reverence for Catholicism, or its systemic stamping-out of the Incan Empire, language, and temples, or Peru's Catholic-controlled government (his words, not mine...I was baptized a crappy cafeteria-Catholic).

He explained his sudden shift in demeanor at the Temple of the Sun; it was apparently subversive in Peru to teach the old ways, even today.

The police were watching and following him.

Then it was Kira and Zadkiel's turn. I waited on tenterhooks as the discourse began.

Zadkiel was relevant, perfect, and love-filled (funny, too). Then suddenly, He announces that a galactic collective-consciousness that had never spoken to anyone before (besides Sri and Kira once) and had been preparing (Kira included) for eons to connect with humanity since its creation, was going to pop-in to say hello.

Oh, maaaaan!

Every hair follicle on my body stood on end as though I had waited for this moment for eons too. As though someone said, "I have an advance copy of the new Star Wars trilogy shot with intense J.J Abrams genius a year before everyone else gets to see it." Zadkiel mentioned that their energy would be so high that He could not return that night.

Just as I was about to ponder the depth of the significance from that pronouncement *by an Archangel*, I witnessed the most relevant spiritual event that my heart carries to this day.

I will remember forever the energy that crashed through my body, and Being, in the moments following.

Every one of us gasped, and half of us immediately began sobbing (myself included) as the Benevolent Ones, from God knows where (literally), spoke their message of Love to us.

A homesickness I'd never experienced before lingered with me long after we all later embraced one another in tears, float-walking to my comfortable bed for a dreamless sleep, and upon greeting the new day.

To my dismay, we all had to wake-up super early (I'm not a morning person) to travel to our next hotel destination to check-in and explore a local rural market. It sounded like it was located in the middle of nowhere, even within the boundaries of the obscure Urubumba Valley. A few porters, beaming at us and leading the way through a winding dirt trail, pushed open a vast set of wooden doors, and my jaw fell open.

Contained within these gates was nothing short of the most incredible hotel-ashram-villas I'd ever, or probably will ever, set foot in. The first thing I noticed, however, were three small (5' or shorter) Incan men dressed in the most Incan-est clothes you'd ever seen, sitting on the green grass. Like out of a movie. They hardly paid us any notice as we all filed past, noting their tremendous energy and presence.

Sri and Kira mentioned to us that they had traveled for three days through the Andes from their village located Buddha-knows-where, to perform an ancient ritual called a Panchamama ceremony with us three days following. I was filled with wonder and visceral anticipation at the honor being done to us.

Speaking of wonderment, I could go on for pages about the paradisian hotel we were to stay at several times during this journey, but I'll do my best to sum-up the many incredible characteristics and history that it possessed.

There were seven sacred, meticulously planted gardens that correlated to each chakra of the human body to meditate in, housing rare flowers from around the planet, many of which could only grow in their native isolated environments... and this place. The intricately laid stone paths, and the many stones inlaid within and without the building structures were unearthed during the land's cultivation for construction, every detail considered.

The South African owner and creator of this sanctuary describes how she, after years of traveling the local area and studying with many pacco's (shaman), had purchased this once barren, unused land because of its energetic centerpiece: A 500-year-old tree who's fruit had fed the last Incan Emperor himself.

All of the wood and stone used as building materials for the impressive two-story bungalows with vaulted ceilings, and even the furniture had either been cultivated from the purchased land or brought from the nearby village.

Our meals were beyond organic (though any vegan knows the FDA has relegated the meaning of that word to a sad joke), the ingredients picked from the gardens by the hands of the only family, and their cousins, to have ever worked there (our same smiling porters). Trust in this family and their honor was beyond question, as there were no locks at this inn, and many of them helped to pridefully construct it. No worries here.

My words can't encapsulate the silent beauty and sacred presence that this place held, but I still dream about the place sometimes. To me, it's an archetype we have sacrificed in our modern culture: Living and listening to the land and each other. *Really* listening, and then caring about what you hear.

After dropping off our bags, we got back on the bus to travel to the ruins of P'isaq where incredible Incan terraces and ruins were constructed into the mountainside like an enormous staircase. We hiked after Don Ruben to another obscure Temple of the Sun, learning from him its hidden history and leading us through powerful group meditations.

A couple of us found a few stone edifices shaped almost like thrones, and when sitting in them, strong currents of energy shot-up my spinal column. We all kept taking turns like we were children at Disneyland, toning and acting like the New-Agey weirdoes that we proudly were.

Exhilarated by our long hike through the ruins, we all returned to the inn to explore its splendor, or to take a nap to process the experience. I chose to meditate in front of the ancient tree, its trunk and branches adorned with many crystals and other respect-offerings left by previous guests. I could feel its grandmotherly energy smiling down on me, and I experienced a healing release connected to my issues of shame about being broke all of the time.

I hadn't realized that it was okay, or even possible to lead an advanced spiritual existence and enjoy financial abundance. Visions of helping thousands of other people to live a life of plenty flashed through my head, and my heart swelled. I now knew I had permission, even if I had no idea how to create it for myself. Thanks Mother.

Dinner was so vegetarian that it was more akin to eating energy, but the cooks were incredible and creative. I meditated again in one of the sacred gardens before turning in.

Early (sigh) in the morning we grabbed our stuff to board the bus that would take us to our train to Aguas Calientes, the valley town at the base of Machu Picchu that we'd be staying at. (I know. I half expected to see John Candy and Steve Martin, eyes rolling, to be sitting next to me too).

When we arrived at Aguas Calientes, famous for its hot springs as the name might suggest, we had to hike up a 30° incline that the town's main road, shops, and hotels were situated upon. Like Diagon Alley lifted on a car-jack.

Our senior pilgrims took a little while to reach the hotel lobby, and I hauled as much of their luggage as I could carry, having never replaced a hip. We finally arrived, dropped-off our stuff, and met in the lobby for a brief lesson about Picchu by Don Ruben before we were to ascend the mountain by bus the next day.

I was close to losing my mind with excitement, like a magnet was pulling me irresistibly toward this spiritual citadel.

After barely sleeping, I zombie-walked to where my group was meeting for breakfast and last minute preparations. We attacked the hotel buffet, which was awesome by the way. The bus ride itself turned out to be an adventure, and a little scary too.

The winding, unpaved road to the world-famous ruins looked juuuuust wide enough for one bus to travel on, until I saw another bus returning down the same path toward us. Our driver slowed, and like the Knight Bus, magically squeaked by, and I was sure half of our vehicle was hanging off of the side of the mountain road, supported by Peruvian miracles.

I couldn't look out the bus. The two drivers could have kissed without leaning out their windows. I prayed a lot. Then we passed (thank God!) and arrived at the top.

This day at Picchu, our group was to receive an intricate, guided tour from Don Ruben, and the day after was supposed to be our free day to explore the temple-city. The first thing we all noticed was that there were no handrails. Anywhere. More than a few less-coordinated travelers have lost their lives to the many potential sheer drop-offs. Thank God for Tai Chi and massage school!

The first remarkable spot that our group came to a halt at were these two circle-shaped formations that rose two inches from the floor as moon craters look. Don Ruben explained that scholars mistook them as ceremonial bowls or something, but then he took out his water bottle and poured it out into them (even though they were roped-off). He invited us to gaze at them from a marked spot on the floor, and we were amazed to discover that it was a means of observing the sun and moon's reflection and position without straining the eyes.

I looked up and saw Kira Raa, Sri Ram Kaa, and one of my fellow travelers arm in arm, *staring wide-eyed at the high noon sun without blinking, for at least five minutes.* WTF! I thought. What freaking planet were these people from?!

We walked down another path and saw a group of lamas (who functioned as Picchu's lawnmowers and landscapers) trotting toward us. All of us moved respectfully aside to let them pass, but then one stopped in front of me.

After regarding me, it presented its hindquarters to me (stuck his ass in my face), and I just automatically placed a hand on its sacrum. It felt twisted, like the lama had landed on it funny, and while I listened neutrally (Craniosacral) its low back twitched very rapidly. When my hand floated off of her/him, I swore that it smiled at me before sauntering off after its group.

Definitely one of the coolest sessions I've ever done.

Don Ruben led us into a chamber where the stones were curved to catch the wind and channel it into the room. The temperature felt at least ten degrees cooler here, and he explained that this was the Incan food storage facility at Picchu.

Brilliant, I thought.

In a nearby room, he sat us against the perfectly articulated stone walls (no mortar used), put a bottle of yellow fluid to his lips, and blew a mist into our faces. Eyes closed, I felt my mind reach into my past for what this intoxicating aroma reminded me of; like a once-visited, beloved candy store you forgot in your youth. The fluid's scent made me light-headed as we all were invited to smile at the Universe; the wall's current flowing through me.

This process was repeated in several other rooms, the meditation-ceremonies becoming progressively deeper and my heart chakra expanding to the point that I secretly began to fear the organ might burst from my chest.

It was deeper than the physical heart though, and my turreted, subconscious armaments and walls crumbling down felt unbearable at times. I witnessed many wounds incurred and received in this lifetime, many long forgotten, however I showed up to grow and heal, so I faced it gratefully.

When we arrived at Picchu's stone quarry, where the countless tons of stone used for its construction were hewn, I found-out why it was such a powerful place. Every enormous stone was composed of feldspar, mica, and quartz (mostly quartz). I was told that the feldspar and mica were used in the local region for heart-oriented spiritual purposes, and quartz is an amplifier and conductor of any energy associated or entrained within it (like a blank computer disk).

Imagine what your being feels like standing atop and within over 100,000 tons of that.

Damn is right.

After about our ninth meditation, I was fried. I could have stayed longer, but I was overloaded and craving a nap, so I took the next bus down to my hotel. I'd be returning tomorrow anyway, and that, with an archangelic channeling to look forward to.

I woke-up three hours later, determined to embrace oblivion in the hot springs, but the amazing crystal shops distracted me. One of the more affluent members of our group took pity on me and handed me a hundred bucks. I burned with shame, while simultaneously craving to impulse-buy a thousand things that caught my eye.

Man, it'd be awesome to be rich, I thought. I had to pace myself, but I still bought a few incredibly beautiful crystals at Peruvian prices. God bless a strong fiat currency!

The next day, we enjoyed a buffet breakfast at the hotel (roughing-it, like I said) as we took the bus back to Picchu. It was our free day to explore, but before we were turned loose, we were to meet for a brief lesson at the backside of the stone quarry with Professor Zadkiel. No freakin' complaint here!

Most of His amazing message pertained to the unity within creation, to appreciate the divinity and perfection even within the supposed mundane. No higher or lower. That ascension was a process of reconnection and remembrance.

Also, that reconnection began and expanded through our re-identification with our crystalline heart.

All beautiful teachings, while overlooking one of the most breathtaking valleys and chain of mountains I'd ever laid eyes upon. Unforgettable (thank Goodness).

We all parted, in awe of our incredible blessings, to run around as children in an amusement park. I saw my companions throughout the day, OM-ing with crystals in their hands to whatever version of Source they prayed to, or holding a pair of those same cylindrical objects Sri and Kira held at their workshop and before channelings.

'They're called Egyptian Healing Rods,' said one of the ladies. 'Here, hold them.' I put the copper (Sun) rod in my right hand, as she showed me, and the silver (Moon) rod in my left. The effect was immediate and amazing.

'That's the most powerful kind there is, cause they make them at different strengths, but as you're an energy guy, there'll be no problem with you using them.'

'Huh?' was all I could manage to say as my meridians throbbed and my crown chakra exploded. The only thought I could coherently focus on was, 'How much,' and 'Where do I buy a pair?'

'Sri and Kira are the national distributors of them because they're friends with the scientist in Russia who figured-out how to make them. It's the only place they're made, too.'

My life had a singular directive and focus when I returned home: Egyptian Healing Rods.

At...all...cost.

I very reluctantly handed them back and thanked her for the revelation.

As I hiked all over the ruins, one of my favorite discoveries was hearing the chattering excitement of over fifty different languages. Picchu truly drew visitors from all over the world, and the desire of humanity's yearning for connection shone like a beacon. A spiritual U.N. for seekers from all races.

I waved at a few Korean brothers and gave high-fives to perceptive Swedish sisters.

So, so cool. Everyone should visit at least once in their life. It's a playground for all of God's children.

Elated, I returned to Aguas Calientes for a little last-minute exploration, and almost passed-by a doorway I hadn't noticed before when I stopped dead in my tracks. An enormous poster of Saint Germain's image stared back at me. I drifted into the coolest metaphysics store I've ever seen to this day, ensnared by the wafting aroma of burning Nag Champa (Sai Baba's) incense and Palo Santo wood.

The wizened owner of the shop smiled at my open-mouthed face. There was an enormous three-tiered altar in the store's center with a pictorial likeness of every angel and ascended master from every culture, and even a few I'd never seen before. Ceremonial pipes and feather bundles, candles and incense burning everywhere.

I spotted the same bottle of yellow fluid Don Ruben used in ceremony with us, and it was for sale! I eagerly bought one and a package of the heart-opening holy wood. I just wanted to curl-up and never leave. Crystals as large as a head or an arm.

This place was straight out of Diagon Alley.

I bowed to the woman before I left, blessing her divinity, and she nodded her acknowledgement. ¡Viva Peru!

With a gratitude I'd never known, my fellow pilgrims and I took the train back to the Urubumba Valley where our paradisian inn awaited us yet again.

We were bused to the Temple of the Wind, and as you might suspect...windy. At one of the observation points you could lean into the wind and let your body go and it would mostly support your weight as it came screaming up the face of the mountain.

It was cool, but I was eager to return to the hotel because it was cooler. Plus, there was the authentic Incan Earth-Mother ceremony to look forward to later.

When we arrived back at the inn, those three holy men (who looked like they hadn't moved an inch) now displayed bracelets, prayer beads, scarves, and a few of their hand-woven hats with colorful tassels on top (for lack of a better term). They'd brought with them from their village to sell us. The inn's owners said that any monetary contribution had a huge economic impact on their people, as they rarely traveled beyond their borders for supplies in a town.

There was an instantaneous blur of wallets, cash, and a near-stampede to relieve them of their wares. I was almost elbowed in the face by a very saintly woman more than once.

One of the wizards stared at me, and I vibrated. He lifted his hand, and in it was my favorite hat to this day. I look ridiculous in it and I love it.

I've done every Reiki attunement while wearing it because it's my wizard hat. Bestowed by an actual wizard.

I gave him almost the rest of my spending money, thinking, screw it, I'll drink water the rest of the trip. I love this hat.

As the sun fell, we were led into a beautifully constructed, octagon-shaped ceremonial ashram, filled with musical instruments and spiritual objects. The senior pacco of the three did a ceremonial offering to Panchamama, the Earth Goddess, and to the Apo, or male mountain spirits. We were asked to formulate our own blessing intentions to be included within his prayer bundle.

It was amazing to witness and to participate within, as well as make music with them around a fire as its conclusion. I sang without restraint, toning whatever sounds my subconscious would allow through the gates of my being.

Kira then surprised us all by informing us that Zadkiel wished to speak to us to offer an ascension acceleration and to answer personal questions we might have.

I felt like I was dreaming!

I timidly raised my hand and asked what my spiritual mission or destiny was (I thought, what the hell, why not go big?). The archangel's reply surprised me very much as the energy bored into me through Kira's eyes.

Zadkiel said that I had major and important training and learning to undergo. That by the end of the cycle of becoming and integration, that the energy and being I would yield would be (pause) 'Oh, Baby!'

Oh, baby? What the…?

I thought the answer was a bit obscure, but that's Spirit's prerogative. It excited me to no limit, though.

I wonder what He meant? I pondered restlessly, still buzzing from the ceremony and information. Everyone had stared over at me, looking impressed and like they wondered the same thing. Naturally, I could hardly sleep that night at all.

I wish I had slept better, because, of course, we had to awaken early for the big day. The reason for why we were here. Ascension-portal-anchoring-day.

I wasn't the only bedraggled pilgrim, though. A few of my brethren had been enjoying explosive diarrhea, as Peruvian microorganisms snuggled into their new intestinal real estate. I was secretly glad that I hadn't tried every vegetable at every restaurant or buffet that I came across.

The ceremony, for which we would receive instruction when we arrived at the destination, would be held at an archeological site known as the Circle of Moray. I had no idea what to expect, rather, I felt a deepening hope that I might play my part with integrity. When we arrived by bus, our group was further impressed by the spiritual ingenuity and creativity of this Incan place of ceremony.

The Circle of Moray was nestled in a small valley and were a set of many concentric rings, set by stone as at Pisaq, each ring at least a man's height. To descend to the next successive ring level, stone outcroppings serving as stairs were set seamlessly into the wall.

It was an impressive view from the top of the hill looking down. We carefully, and with sacred awe of the expanding moment, hiked to the inner circle to...well, Kira instructed us step by step.

I can't give the full recounting here of the exact process for anchoring the ascension portal, but it involved Tanzanite and would have looked trippy as hell to an outsider. We, of course, were caught-up in the bliss of the moment, but I could tell by Don Ruben's politely incredulous expression afterward, that we had looked crazy.

Well, bless it, that's why it's called the *New* Age. I know it was powerful (at least for me) for several reasons.

My grandmother, my beloved Nana, and matriarch of our family had passed five days before I had left for the trip. I had had to choose between following my heart or familial obligation and funeral attendance. That had sucked.

After the ceremony concluded, I looked behind and above me and saw her in her 30 year-old form, smiling down on me and being honored by countless celestial beings for her well-lived life and for the service I was now doing for Spirit. I finally cried after that.

Secondly, in a huge group hug, we all started staring at the sun. I was no longer afraid of it blinding me, and though a few tears spilled, I could finally gaze upon our Life-source without blinking. I stared for at least a minute at this beautiful disk, and haven't been able to do it since that day at that position in the sky. I'll have to begin practicing at sunset again. It was worth recovering that energetic connection.

Thirdly, as my group continued to sun-gaze, I looked behind me again, and saw the calling-card afro of my Beloved Guru of Gurus, Satya Sai Baba, peeking out and moving amongst our huddling group hug. His Holy Presence among us was an unspeakable honor to me, and my heart filled to overflowing at the magnitude of so many divine blessings. I felt a completeness bordering on death, or maybe the relief of being born; I'm not sure which.

The journey began to take-on a dream-like quality after the ceremony. When we returned to the Hotel Libertador in Cuzco, we discovered that Hurricane Rita had begun to pound the U.S.'s coastline (Zadkiel mentioned many Earth changes for three years following the portal anchoring, because of planetary clearing and cleansing).

Before we left Cuzco for Lima, though, we went out to dinner, and I made the unfortunate mistake (though I was honored) to sit next to Kira Raa.

This Lady can practically photosynthesize light, and I hadn't eaten any meat for about a week. I put a little of everything at this buffet, from guinea pig (a bit bony and gamey) to alpaca (a type of lama that grows wool as a sheep does). Try something new as a first time world traveler, right?

As I was about to tuck in, one of the travelers across from me, clutching her heart, asks, 'You eat *flesh?*'

'Um, excuse me?' I asked.

I was getting pretty tired of getting lectured on diet, especially when many of the plant-munching purists looked about as strong and healthy as a recovering hospital patient. 'Yeah I do. I prayed for the release of the animal's suffering and am now welcoming it to become one with my form. The plant life you're consuming suffered horribly and with zero ceremony on the way to your plate; I'm imagining that you hardly care because it didn't have a face.'

I began to eat with gusto, not realizing that Kira's nauseated facial expression next to me stemmed from the fact that she and Sri lived on a *lama ranch* in New Mexico. A coyote had killed one of her beloved lamas before the trip, and I was basically eating one of her children whilst sitting next to her.

I felt like Bush's Vice President, so I quickly got another plate heaped with vegetables.

When we got back to Lima, I found out on CNN that there had been crazy electrical storms in my native San Diego. While I watched that report in my fourth-story hotel room, a 7.4 earthquake rocked Lima, as well as my hotel building. That sucked.

I hollered in my head, 'Do you folks mind backing-off a bit until I'm safely back at home?!' I heard laughter and received an, 'It ain't about you, Buck-o!' feeling, 'but thanks for the input.'

Smart-ass angels.

I arrived back at LAX with great relief (bags and all), but with an even greater sense of anticipation, if it was possible. This dream journey seemed impossible in so many ways, but it happened just as I described it. Its still feels beyond description.

I finished integrating my Shamballa Master/Teacher attunement, returned from a spiritual mission in Peru, did ceremonies with shaman (sorry, Don Ruben, paccos), talked to an Archangel, stared at the sun, and had (easily) quit smoking in less than a month.

Good month. One of my best ever.

I hadn't the foggiest idea how my life could possibly get any stranger, or how I might access greater power and qualitative betterment, but as you're beginning to know how this goes…of course I asked anyway.

Thanks Zadkiel! I've never stopped or could ever thank Him enough for his cryptic encouragement or loving messages.

Chapter 11

Returning to, and living in San Diego took on a fairly surreal flavor. Having been raised in an upper-middle-class family there all of my life, and then swinging idly from the lowest rung of the socioeconomic food-chain had taught me much about value, what's really important in my life, and that Joy could be attained no matter what.

Observing the Peruvian farmworkers toiling over potato fields at 11,000 feet with a fourteen-hour smile on their face deepened that understanding for me.

As Don Ruben oft repeated to our entourage, *work* was considered a curse word in the Quechua language. The people *played* with the land all day.

I embraced this philosophy with relish at the massage clinic, playing with bodies, stresses, or energies. I enjoyed the clients and myself immensely, but my mind would persistently wonder, 'What's next? Are we going to serve in this manner forever? Hey, what the hell is going on?!'

Most therapists in the massage industry only receive a percentage of what a client will pay a clinic or spa, and I was thankful to receive what I did. But there's little growth potential (wages-wise), regardless of an increasing skill-set or burgeoning expertise. Often, by the time a practitioner has built their private practice to the point of self-employment, their hands or shoulders give-out, or they enjoy the chaos of feast and famine cycles of activity at their office.

I enjoyed the pseudo-stability that being someone's employee can bring (though you're still at the mercy of the business aptitude of one's management team, or owners) but I couldn't envision a future there. I'd become adept at treading financial water and had mastered surviving, but for the first time in my adult life, I'd discovered a yearning for the abundant life. The feeling of having more than just enough.

Mahatma Gandhi, an Oxford-educated lawyer at one time, who became the greatest political and spiritual leader for change in the 20th century, died with about $5 in possessions. Ditto for Jesus (royalty from the House of David) and Buddha (former prince). You'll notice however, that their cultures' audiences were impoverished.

Would the masses have responded as they had if these figureheads approached them, in those cultures, at those times, clothed in royalty or aristocracy? I personally doubt it. It hardly makes sense to make people less than you if your goal is to empower them to activate their innate Divinity. Jesus *made a point* to ride a mule into town.

However, I was a contemporary mystic living in one of the more expensive cities in the U.S. in the 21st century. Peru had introduced me to international travel, 4 and 5-star accommodations, and spiritual people who were beyond financially free. Sure, I could become another penniless teacher (there are plenty of them), claiming that this asceticism brings me closer to Source and teaching others to do likewise (for a nominal donation, of course).

This, despite the fact that the Law of Attraction, and all spiritual writings profess that God *abundantly* provides (as exemplified in nature), and it is His pleasure to deliver the goods (kingdom). The Good Book says *mansions* in heaven, not shacks. Mom and Dad are *ballers*.

The vision I had at the ancient feet of the Giving Tree at that inn of paradise made me realize that I'd be a hell of a lot more useful to my awakening brothers and sisters in my home culture as a commander of resources, than not. My newly formulated and ongoing hypothesis joyfully became that of utilizing the Laws of God in order to create abundance, and having done so, be able to teach others to free themselves likewise.

I realized that working from the consciousness-plane of duality, competition, and gross materiality (and all attachments pertaining to thereof) would have been the energetic catalyst to my self-destructive demise. Playing with my Higher consciousness in the realms of Oneness, creation, and the spiritual Laws of Mind, I deeply believed, could manifest a lifetime where I could evolve into a master and live Heaven while still here on Earth.

The trick is, how is the game played?

What are the rules?

I've noticed while studying the Law of Attraction/Mind, that most people are really good in several components of it, but lack the proper thinking to manifest what they desire in others. Great health and money, but completely inept with the love life. Excellent at attracting lovers, yet broke as a joke, or in debt. Or highly spiritual, but with poor health, and self-sabotaging through attracting "incidents" or "accidents."

Having never formulated a friendship or relationship with a rich person, I had no idea how they thought and therefore attracted-in wealth. There were a few self-help authors who were spiritual and rich, rewarded for their service to humanity, but they rarely became über-specific about how to do it.

Gratitude seemed to be the universal prerequisite and was brought-up often, but at this point I was a technique-hound; I could carve-out the artistry of it all once I understood the dynamics a little deeper.

Then a pyramidal book-pile at Barnes and Noble came through for me yet again (don't forget, this is before I discovered the beloved Amazon.com...but I digress). The pale gold covers of T. Harv Eker's NY Times No. 1 Best Seller <u>The Secrets of the Millionaire Mind</u>™ stared back at me.

Bingo.

A five-minute perusal of this mind changing/life changing gem was more than enough time for me to see the wisdom in offering $20 as a tithe for a brighter today and future.

The first half of Harv's book evaluated, with stark references, how the Law of Attraction and Mind had *everything* to do with a person's monetary experience. Perfectly.

The second half of SMM, with little reverence and all respect, examines the seventeen ways that rich folks and poor folks think differently and so achieve opposing monetary results.

The book will be a modern classic, I am sure, and should be a mandatory freshman economics text in high school or college. From cover to cover, I kept saying, 'Ohhhhh meekrab, I wish I'd known all this ten years ago.'

A friend of mine who grew-up in an abundant-less household, was so offended by the rich and poor mentality comparisons, that they set out to purchase the book that very evening, with the same indignation as I had with the book about stopping smoking.

All we could discuss the next day was about how spot-on Harv was with every meticulous assessment of how our mental habits and biases shape the outcome of our material experience.

What was so especially amazing about this particular book was that it included a free invitation to attend a Millionaire Mind Intensive seminar. With the purchase of his book, you got a ticket to a three-day event whose cost was the equivalent of over $1,300 per person. At first I thought it was bull-pucky, but I looked it up online, and sure enough, the seminar cost about $1,500 out-of-pocket after paying a materials fee.

I had already gleaned much from the book and was doing the mental exercises daily, when my once-incredulous friend expressed her desire to check it out for herself. The closest seminar was going to be held in Denver, so we got some cheap plane tickets, paid the $90 materials fee, and booked a youth-hostel room for three days.

What really blew my mind was that Sonny had only heard me *talk* about the book, bought one, and without having read it, decided that he was going to fly out there to change his mental programming around money too. Talk about faith!

I should mention here that, being a San Diego native, I'm not a huge fan of the cold. It had snowed for a solid, record-setting three straight weeks before we flew into Denver, so I prayed and desperately imagined dragging the California sunshine with me.

The sky, thankfully, was a beautiful blue every time that we stepped outside of the Denver Convention Center to view the Rockies, my favorite North-American Apo. (Though it did, at times, dip to 30 freaking degrees several times...this is Arctic conditions to a native Southern Californian!).

The seminar, most unfortunately, was held daily from 8am to 6pm, and one of the days was *twelve hours*. It truly was an intensive seminar, but I wondered what Harv's people could offer that could possibly merit a near $1,500 price tag? I received the beginning of the answer to that question the moment that I approached the huge room slated for the event.

Two rows of bright-eyed, grinning, beaming, staff-shirt-wearing maniacs were herding the participants through the double doors, enthusiastically high-fiving everything in sight. These folks looked like they'd downed electricity smoothies for breakfast. One older woman almost slapped my hand clean off.

As I walked through the doors to several more 'Woo-Hoo's!' and 'Alllriiiight's!' I looked up on stage, and about fifty folks of all ages were boogying their asses off to some 80's song (I forget which one, as I try my best to disassociate my mind from hair-bands and crotch-high Italian shorts) and having the time of their lives.

When the songs ended and we all found our seats (it looked packed with over 1,200 seats), one of the presenters started firing up the crowd, getting people to shout abundance affirmations from the book, or just shouting and clapping in general. It hadn't even started yet and I was pooped, but I was determined to go full-throttle the whole time. I'd come all this way to change my thinking, and dammit, I was going to.

I almost had cheered myself hoarse when the main presenter, Doug, took the stage to officially kick-off the seminar. I glanced into the "materials goodie bag" given to us at the beginning, and was stunned at how much stuff we'd been handed. The course folder and seminar workbook were beautifully put together, we got a CD *case* worth of self-help instruction interviews from not only Harv, but many other multimillionaires, and a sweet-looking seminar tote bag to boot.

Usually, giveaways look lame and cheap, but you could tell a lot of thought went into it. I'd guess it had better if some folks just shelled-out 15-hundo.

Doug was an amazing presenter and human being in general. He'd survived blowing himself up during a gas-leak explosion in his basement (says he's now an *adamant* non-smoker), recovered from his massive 3rd degree burns and thought, heck, I'm gonna become a multimillionaire. And did it. Harv's teachings helped him to get there, so now he's teaching the seminar for him. Sounded good to me.

We screamed, danced, mingled, affirmed, and anchored every positive wealth mantram into our subconscious minds. We forgave our parents (and *their* programming around money), classified and identified our consciousness archetypes relating to money, and uncovered every possible habit, assumption, and nuance we had ever possessed toward wealth.

All of us examined in painstaking detail every precept in SMM, filling-in the missing words in the booklet, then always doing some physical action or exercise to anchor it into our subconscious mind ('till you wanted to beat your brains in...then it was time for lunch). More yelling and cheering to follow.

It dawned on me finally that the cycles of activity, sitting, and shouting were a deliberate attempt to soften our egos' control over our mind so that something new could enter and take root. I thought it was brilliant, but a surprising number of people couldn't handle it, and never returned after the breaks.

Doug mentioned that if doing it our way were working for us, we'd already be millionaires by now. The discomfort is what growth feels like.

Fair point, sensei.

I'll share with you now the two most important things that I came away with from the seminar and book. It boiled down to mostly this:

Money Management. The rich are awesome at it and I sucked at it. No one in school (ironically never mentioned in Economics class) ever taught me how to do it. Mom and Dad...ditto. Harv's system is simple and, I feel, genius. It can be taught to a five-year-old, dividing your money between five accounts with different purposes and percentages.

It's directly related to one's monetary Law of Attraction, because (paraphrasing Harv's words) why should the Universe give you more when you can't responsibly handle a little? It worked so well for me, that using the system, I was able to purchase the Mac computer (my first ever!) that I'm typing this very book upon.

Investments and Passive Income. The great secret of the rich (besides their use of corporations to avoid taxes and legal culpability). You can examine Robert Kiyosaki's work synergistically with Harv's at your discretion for a clearer insight into the "millionaire's mind."

The whole idea is to make money without *having to work to create it.* Acquiring passive income streams and having them making money for you while you sleep is the very essence of becoming financially free.

Not necessarily rich, but free. Once your passive income equals your living and life expenses, a person is free, according to Eker.

"Work" then morphs from an obligatory survival necessity into a game of joyful service for humanity and Earth; an expression of divinity (or energy) because you *choose* to, not *have* to.

This is the power of investments and managing what we already have. This is the power of gratitude, responsibility, and admitting that we may not know everything; to have the courage to laugh at ourselves and try something completely new. My life, it seems, always improves when I embrace this consciousness, and it has noticeably in my financial life.

I would have gladly paid $1,500 for the experience I had in Denver, if I'd possessed it at the time. Of course, if I were already rich, I'd know how to write it off my taxes as an educational business expense from one of my (non-existent) C-corporations, but I'm not quite there yet! I stress *yet*.

The most profound metamorphosis I witnessed wasn't even within myself; it was in my best friend Sonny. Not only had he absorbed every concept taught at the seminar, he actually began to help others clarify *their* understanding of how thought relates to created reality, as though he'd known this stuff for years.

Seminar participants I'd never interacted with would approach me, and seeing that I was with him, would congratulate me on having found such an astute mentor. I couldn't have been more pleased, and we laughed about it many times together.

On our breaks, we came up with numerous wonderful ideas on how to create businesses that would serve the Light, the planet, humanity, and liberate our family and friends from financial bondage.

Many of them were too intricate and vast to accomplish without the influence and monetary contributions of investors, but both of us could foresee the likelihood of meddling and the energetic dilution that would ultimately create self-serving corporate entities with little regard for humanity or Earth.

How does one build from the ground floor up, so that we may have the influence to guide our larger projects?

Then Harv gave us the idea.

Sonny often amazed me with the details of his daughters' upbringing, and the parental philosophies he employed to accomplish the feat. I'd never heard of such methods of communication and decision-making used with children, much less achieving the results he had.

He didn't hit them, yell at them, or even have to punish them! And the girls were world-class people (as previously mentioned). 'How did you do it?' I'd often ask, knowing how many parental struggles so many folks that I knew faced daily. 'Could you teach it to others?'

'Sure, my man,' he'd reply with his trademarked grin. 'It's easy. We invented a family game when the girls were little to teach them self-reliance and self-responsibility, so they'd be completely prepared for the world when they reached adulthood. They learned the habits young, then it carries over easily.'

'Dude,' I eloquently replied, '*You* need to write a book about this stuff. Parents are fiending for this kind of info. Dr. Spock only goes so far, bro.'

We had visions of book signings, family consultations, huge seminars, and even an appearance on The Daily Show (we've got to think big, right Harv?). He could meet the needs of possibly millions of people, serve the Light, and make passive income.

He'd never written a book before, and English was his third language, but who cares? If Harv and hundreds of other self-help authors could do it, why couldn't he? I promised him that I'd lend whatever help I could if he ever decided to give it a go. Then, of course, I'd forgotten all about it when we returned to California.

However, months later, he calls me and proclaims his book created.

'Huh?' I forgetfully inquired.

'I wrote it man! But I need your help to make it look like a book.'

When I inspected and read it, it was a long, but beautiful block of story that required my experience of having read a thousand books. I knew what a good, great, crappy, best-selling, highly forgettable, classic, or 'I wish I had that time back' book looked like, having been a prolific reader.

So, I broke the story down into where I thought the subjects began or ended, creating chapters, and helped come up with cool-sounding titles for them.

Then I set about the enjoyable task of editing; re-wording what I felt the words were trying to convey, but keeping it sounding like Sonny's voice was telling the tale.

The most mind-blowing revelation I had, besides how truly amazing my best friend and his life were, was how easy it was to create a book. I had a blast assisting him, and realized halfway through that someday soon, I'd be writing my own.

Many of my clients who had mined my personal history and spiritual information for years had asked me to write one, clarifying concepts for them or directing them to resources for expanded self-exploration.

Well, a book, I realized, was a bunch of (about) ten page essays or topics of related information stacked upon one another (chapters) with an introduction of varying length, a catchy title, and a references page or section to avoid lawsuits.

I've just decided to include my sources' names and titles of their works to give them props here, but if I've forgotten anyone, please don't be a dick and sic your lawyer(s) on me. I'll be glad to revise the next edition with my humblest apologies. Sonny's book turned-out amazing, and though he self-published, I have no doubt that it could change the way children are raised, worldwide, for the better.

He's a rare man with an incredible story to tell, and his techniques are reproducible. Everyone who has read <u>A Success Story of a Single Parent</u> has written him to express how it had deeply affected him or her.

Sonny's courage gave me the courage to write what you've read here, though I doubt I could convey with words the strength of his character and how it affects everyone whom he meets. He's kind of like Uzumaki Naruto sans the ninjutsu.

If anyone deserves to make it, to free himself financially, I pray that this man amongst men does, and I know he will. So can you and I.

Bless you, brother, and bless you Harv.

Chapter 12

So you may be rightfully wondering, whereforartthou wizardry? Where's my quantum dish (now served cold)? Why have I endured eleven chapters of pseudo-interesting, though mildly entertaining, spiritual pandering?

To which I reply, fair point.

To the imitation-meat of it! (For my vegan homies).

If you ever do have the wisdom to purchase or download <u>An Ascension Manual</u> by Serapis, you'll find within its pages a descriptive miracle. A boiled-down, perfect explanation of the holographic nature of reality, from the nature of consciousness and how it relates to creation, as well as Energy's physics, or dynamics from the quantum to the gross "physical" level.

Ditto for the masterpiece <u>Busting Loose From the Money Game</u> by Robert Scheinfeld. To put it simply, reality as we know and experience it is a **hologram**.

Like the visionary Gene Roddenberry's holodeck on Star Trek's flagship The Enterprise (TNG, of course), our physical world that our brains are bio-chemically decoding as objects of mass or matter, is actually vibrating waves of energy, sometimes densified to the degree of becoming particles, or "solid reality."

Physicists in today's world base their reality model by how Isaac Newton postulated the objectified world behaved, or Newtonian Physics. Experiments involving Newtonian models measured and observed the behavior of objects that were 1/1000th of an inch or bigger, from rocks, to planets. They *believed* that everything fit this model.

Scientists in about the late 19th century, however, began to rebel against this blanket description, because the "solid" objects they were measuring were discovered to be mostly empty space and condensed energy moving at incredible speeds.

As Serapis describes, if the nucleus of an atom were a football that was placed upon the center of the fifty-yard line, then the first orbital field of electrons would be in the tenth row of seats in the stadium! And every field of electrons might be 50 rows apart. The next atom in a molecule might be in the next town over! That's a huge space-to-solid-stuff differential!

Note, I said electron field, not particle. The reason for this is that when an atom was photographed unobserved, the electron would form a cloud, or every possible position it *could* be in, and when observed, would densify into the traditionally high-speed particle it's been assumed to be.

So the scientists debated; is the electron a particle or wave? To which you may rightly ask, 'Who cares?'

Well, a bunch of guys and a few gals in white lab coats who enjoy pondering the nature of reality. The 'what is it, and how does it work' question (minus the why...that's been separated into metaphysics -- or the physics of the heart). Scientists seem to be the western world's acknowledged yogis, except the science is objectified and measured by machines, instead of internalized experimentation measured by subjective consciousness.

Science, and quantum physics in particular, has been busy for a century and a half, verifying with data and mathematical models what saints and sages have been saying for millennia. All particles can be broken down to the tiniest unit of light, called quarks. The Torah says essentially the same thing, that the Creator used Light to create this universe.

An atom is just a probability field until someone observes it, collapsing it into a "something," or particle. Quantum physicists call this occurrence *the collapse of the wave function*. The Law of Mind and Attraction says that our thoughts become objects in reality, that everything is just condensed thought.

Why is this relevant?

Well, it means you're creating your reality from the quantum level (1/1000th of an inch or smaller). Your thoughts and observations theoretically program the personal 'holodeck' of your life. It means you really are (probably) a magical, reality-shifting being, but have more than likely been creating your life through limiting programming or access due to your **beliefs** *of what reality really is or actually works.*

The working hypothesis is this: Observations made (qualitatively) and subsequent thoughts offered in response to them, shaped the fabric of reality! (There are not a few spiritual masters in India and Tibet rolling their eyes right now in a no-shit-Bennedict Cumberbatch-like fashion).

It will be done unto you as you believe. (Jesus)

All we are is the result of what we have thought. (Buddha)

The movie <u>What the Bleep do We Know Anyway?!</u> visually demonstrates in quantum-physical, and biochemical

160

paradigm-terminology, precisely how this happens. How our thoughts create our emotions. How the act of observation determines the nature or dynamics of reality, *subjectively* experienced.

This alludes to how, perhaps, human beings have been able to produce seeming miracles in healing, or other impossible feats by the standards of Newtonian physics (even though Newton, himself, was a mystic and occultist. Look it up.).

Remember in the first chapter, that the catalyst for my entire journey into the unknown domain was *accepting the possibility* It could exist. This shattered my assumptions of "reality" as I knew it to be, producing a consciousness-altering/upgrading event that perhaps could have been experienced at all times, but was filtered-out by my tiny, pin-hole perceptive apparatus labeled "conscious mind."

How is this useful to you or me?

These, and all quantum descriptions of reality have only been useful for proving that Spirit is the only explanation for the intricate perfection of everything, and all that we experience through Being.

That's right, I said it.

Who cares, right? Mental masturbation, right?

Until one day...

I'm flipping through a local New-Agey-type magazine at a café and see an advertisement for a seminar in healing, offered by a doctor from Seattle.

Nice glamour shot buddy!

My smirk turned into a scoff after reading the description of his quantum-based technique, called Matrix Energetics.

Instant results.

It's easy.

Go beyond the 'healing paradigm' and *sending energy* (like Reiki).

Balls, I thought. The balls on this guy.

I gave it no greater thought until my (now ex) girlfriend went to his seminar in L.A. a month or two later and was raving about her experiences.

Really? I thought. Show me.

She smiled and put her hand on my lower back, and her other hand out in front of my body. Then a wave of energy rolled through my body that truly defies verbal description (but I'll try anyway). It was sort of like the quality of holding space as a big shift happened during Craniosacral Therapy, but more instantaneous and dynamic. Like the moment one experiences right before fainting.

Holy shit, and of course, WTF!

I instantly and intuitively knew it was the most powerful technique or approach to energy available to mankind, period. I almost collapsed, physically and bodily, as she continued to laughingly administer what she'd learned.

Not only was it the most energetically powerful...*anything* that I had experienced by way of technique or system, but I was able to learn its basic tenets within five minutes and could successfully return the waving sensation to her, experiencing its effects in my own body as she doubled over.

Of course, I had now a singular motive for even bothering with the respiratory process at all...

Matrix Energetics.

Attending the Matrix Energetics seminar.

Mastering Matrix Energetics.

BY ANY AND ALL MEANS NECESSARY!!!

Almost needless to say, I mentally flagellated myself for making assumptions about the good doctor's obvious genius and mastery. Gregg Braden used to do the whole Fabio-hair thing, and just look at what he did for clarifying the relationship between Divinity and Physics! Go on, Samson!

That's what you get, Joshua. What did J.C. say about judgment, hmm? Now you'll have to wait three long months for the Matrix Energetics seminar to come back around to Los Angeles.

Bullocks.

A month before the conference, work at the massage clinic ground to a frustrating halt, and I knew Spirit was again testing my resolve.

Um...no-brainer.

Screw paying those bills!

I'll admit, I was still in the throes of self-education (now almost seven years) and lacked the energetic wherewithal to put many of Harv Eker's wealth principles to the test, but I didn't mind surviving just a little while longer. The wealth of Spirit held the entirety of my focus at that moment, and I still deeply knew that all else would be added unto me later.

I had no idea what kind of metaphysical background this doctor had, especially since he'd be teaching his art through the reality-framework of quantum physics, but my intuition (and my ex) alluded to the notion that he was a kindred Spirit. I could've cared less if he were a Martian-atheist-mutant-Neo-Conservative-sociopath.

As long as he could teach me his approach, and didn't eat my liver with fava beans and a good Chianti, I was golden.

The seminar ranged over a four-day period. Friday night was an optional 3-hour demo-and-discussion gathering to introduce ME to the seminar participants, and was a free event for those still on the fence about signing-up for it.

Saturday and Sunday were the meat (sorry vegans) of the seminar, Level One lasting all day until about 5pm. Monday was Level 2, where we'd be doing Allah-knows-what from 9-5pm as well. You know I wasn't about to miss a second of it.

I took my seat on Friday night with zero expectations. Charging onto the stage, the greatest wizard, and teacher I'd ever meet, greeted us all.

He looked nothing like his photograph, at least in essence (perhaps a wonton PR admirer was responsible). A 6'3", leather-jacket-wearing madman stood before us, prowling the stage, his face alight with the blazing energy of a five-year-old with little parental oversight and a sugar high.

He seemed to fill the whole room and smiled at us all like the Son of Hermes he is. We all applauded loudly, as Dr. Richard Bartlett began to introduce us to his universe, and began to take a wrecking-ball to the boundaries of ours.

The guy was hilarious, at that. He seemed to tower over the audience as he offered personal anecdotes regarding the origins of the system. That he was trying to heal his once-sickly young son from chronic pneumonia, pursued a chiropractic and naturopathic doctorate to find the solution, all the while begging the Universe for the power to do something about it.

I personally didn't have that kind of catalyst for acquiring skill-sets (thank Buddha), but it struck a chord in that we both asked for the highest from the Highest.

After finally finding the solution through learning from Dr. Victor Frank, who invented TBM (Total Body Modification), he described how he obsessively studied every energy technique that he could, becoming like a witch-doctor chiropractor with an incredibly successful practice, but no one approach worked universally for him.

Then, after a *massively* sleep-deprived week, Matrix Energetics happened to him.

Now, this is paraphrased from his book <u>Matrix Energetics:</u> <u>The Science and Art of Transformation</u>, but he was seeing a young patient with an eye problem that would probably require surgery. Frustrated with the results he was getting, he asked the Universe for a solution, and he hallucinated that Superman (George Reeves) walked through the wall with his cape a-flappin' in the wind.

Dr. Bartlett, tripping out of his mind, asks George if he can do anything, and Superman beams his x-ray vision into the little girl's affected eye. It had the look of shattered glass. Dr. Bartlett says he imagined what it might have looked like before 'whatever' had shattered, and the little girl convulses on the table, and is effing healed.

Um, WTF did you say?

A hallucination did *what?!*

He smiles at our stunned looks of disbelief, and mentions that we'll cover later the power of interacting with holographic archetypes. The important piece to understand was that he could *voluntarily enter this state of consciousness,* creating healing effects *instantly* because of it with his patients.

Dr. Bartlett's many failed efforts to teach this miraculous "something" to his long-time colleague and frustrated left-brained buddy Dr. Mark Dunn, motivated him to find a frame of reference to explain the unexplainable. He found that the inexplicable was explained quite perfectly in quantum physics.

After making-fun of the now *extremely* right-brained Dr. Dunn a little bit more (who actually helped Dr. Bartlett form, teach, and demonstrate Matrix Energetics in its earlier seminars, and the system itself), he asks a woman in the third row to come onto the stage with him.

While ascertaining that she had a bad left shoulder by roughly palpating (feeling) the difference between the right one, he explains how we're all hallucinating a consensus reality, but one with *limiting physics assumptions*. That the act of our observing, or measuring anything in our reality, and the *consciousness quality that we utilize while doing so*, determines what we experience holographically (as human beings).

Sound familiar?

Then Dr. Bartlett mentions that the 'technique' that he's about to demonstrate is the foundation that the deeper approaches to Matrix Energetics rests upon (and which I'd learned from my ex in about 5 min.).

'You look for a point that's stuck, hard, or rigid, like this lady's shoulder. Then you feel for another point either on or off of the body that makes the first point feel even more rigid (he touches a place where her collar bone meets the sternum).'

'Then draw a line connecting the two points, representing the wave function and our act of measuring with our awareness. Then let those points go in your consciousness, collapsing the wave function.'

When he said the words, 'collapsing the wave,' the lady's shoulder he demonstrated this on not only dropped; so did she. Like she'd just fainted momentarily.

One of the staff I hadn't noticed 'till then had run up on stage behind the waving woman as she fell backward, and caught her. He looked completely nonplussed, as though this happened all of the time, and laid her down gently on the stage to process.

Not only that, but I felt a wave of energy flow through *my* being when this all happened.

Every face in the room, except his, mirrored only one Beatnik exclamation: WOW.

When the lady stood back up with the assistant's, well, assistance, she looked dazed and not a little pleased when Dr. Bartlett flung her once-rigid arm and shoulder around like a puppet, displaying a perfect range of motion. My mouth began to water.

This must be the, 'Oh Baby' thing that Zadkiel had spoken of in Peru. I felt like the luckiest person on Earth to be there; like having backstage passes to a Dave Matthews concert, and having Dave give you one of his guitars just because he's feeling generous, and later singing with him for hours with Carter and the gang. Luckier!

(I know I'm gonna catch hell for that from Dave fans. Not a few people have intimated that they'd be okay with dying after something like that.).

After three hours and many more instantaneously-changing-seminar-participants later (at one point, six writhing or catatonic bodies littered the stage), my whole reality had begun to, again, completely change.

My hands went numb from clapping as he exited the room. Every person looked like they'd just pitched a no-hit Game 7, found Wonka's Golden Ticket, and got to sleep with their dream lover to celebrate. I know that's how I felt. (How Tom Brady must feel all of the time, come to think on it).

I wished that I could just bend, or fast-forward time so I could already be learning from this mad genius.

The dude was *Tesla*. I'll happily coin that adjective.

This was it, the "it" I'd been waiting for, but I'm not sure how I knew it. I just did.

Level One

Even though I tried to arrive early to get a good seat, there were already one hundred and fifty attendees lined outside of the double-doors to the conference hall (morning people!!!). By the time I found an empty chair, I was way to the right of the stage, which had a single massage table set-up toward the back. I began flipping through the seminar notebook and manual that the Matrix Staff had handed-out at the doors.

Before I could take-in any of the material, Dr. Bartlett jumped onto the stage, clapping wildly and waving at us to get up and do likewise, as rock music wailed through the speakers. All attendees young and old, well-dressed or hippied-out began to clap as the good doctor sank into a trance, adjusting the grids and fields of the room with dancing fingers (and occasionally breaking-off a tasty air-guitar riff where the song asked for one). Then he welcomed us to wild applause.

Right off the bat, he did his very best to offend us, or at least our identification with who and what we thought we were, or did, or had learned. Dr. Bartlett asked for everyone with a doctorate level education to please raise their hand. He smiles his maniacal smile, stating that these persons would possibly hate him, and that those with no formal education would probably be better at Matrix.

He'd know, too, because he had two of them, and could also therefore talk as much shit as he pleased.

I already loved the guy. Socrates all over again.

He paced all over the stage for about an hour, poking fun at the Western medical paradigm, its assumptions about physical reality, and how our assumptions have completely boxed-in *our* consciousness. He was here to essentially help us identify where and how we've created those boxes and then, with great joy and playfulness, utterly rip the box to pieces.

Dr. Bartlett then asks us to open our manuals, so we can fill our left-brain intellect with enough information so it will just shut the hell up when we get to the fun stuff. His slide-show presentation was precise and linear.

We began with Descartes, and where spirituality was split from science. Then the rise of classical physics leading toward the creation of relativity theory. Dr. Bartlett explains that when an experiment's results didn't fit the mathematical models or hypothesis, the scientists just dreamed-up a new model to fit the data.

In his words, 'They just made it all up!' This process didn't change as the models reflected relativism, then quantum relationships.

The Big Burrito. Quantum reality(s).

Dr. Bartlett, with unheard-of specificity and clarity explains how every facet of our experienced reality is not really...reality. Not as our individuated, "I"-self consciousness is tracking it, anyway.

That our reality on a quantum level is a 'cloud of potential' until an act of observation (choice) determines the state of its physical actualization.

He points out that physicists agree that this applies at the quantum level, but because they don't *believe* that it can exist on the macro level, *they never observe it.*

Yeah? Do a séance and ask Nikola Tesla's ghost about the Philadelphia Experiment. Or about scalar physics. *Anyway...*

So, at this quantum level, energy is either manifesting as a *particle* (an observed condensation) or a *wave* (unobserved potentiality, or the quantum field). Sometimes these waves overlap and intersect to form patterns of condensation, also creating vibrational layers (dimensions) of our holographic reality.

Pay close attention now, because here comes the important part.

Where two waves are of the same frequency, they add to create larger waves. This is referred to as *summation*. This is the *fundamental dynamic* as to how thoughts theoretically interact within the Law of Attraction: Like attracts like. The more you think it, the more it gets created.

Where waves are exactly opposite, the amplitudes subtract, either completely or partially destroying one another. This is what Dr. Bartlett says, in essence, is what he is doing when he 'un-collapses the wave function.' There is *a lot* to this simple phrase.

According to him, in our holographic reality the interference pattern created by a complex series of wave-fronts (manifesting as multiple variations of imbalances or pathology in our body) can be broken-down into its most basic components, and returned to the perfection inherent within the original creation (Brahma's leela).

Well, how the heck do we do that by observing, or measuring reality with as inept an apparatus as our brains? (The highly educated, at this point, are fairly uncomfortable in their chairs). 'By intention and noticing what we notice!' he booms to the crowd. 'The key is to let go and trust, and if you've forgotten how, then you're going to relearn how to this weekend!'

'Ma'am, can I borrow you?' he asks a woman in the front row.

She was one of those adorable Latina grandmothers. Dr. Bartlett palpates her back and asks her if she's had scoliosis her whole life. She squeaks, 'Si.' 'Can I show the audience?' he asks.

Before she can completely answer, he spins her around, lifts the back of her shirt up, and scrapes his thumbnail down the spinous processes of her spine, leaving a winding red mark to show her obvious curvature deviations.

The moments that followed changed me, and my "healing" practice forever.

Just as he had during his Friday night demo, he explained that he'd be teaching this technique to us all in a few moments, and that it was the foundation to the more complex approaches to Matrix Energetics we'd learn later.

Richard selects his two points along her spine, where his attention is most drawn to (just because that's what he noticed), connected them by drawing a line between them (representing the wave function), then "collapsed the wave."

Before our beloved abuelita collapsed to the floor to process/integrate (350 people gasping), I saw *with my waking eyes* the vertebrae in her spine move into alignment. I saw them physically move, real time, I shit you not.

As she collapsed to the floor, writhing, screaming, and laughing hysterically, I stood up onto my chair to see her better. I caught eyes with the wizard-whom-spoke-doctor-speak, and we shared a moment roughly comparable to introducing a friend to Pink Floyd on their first mushroom trip: Dark Side of the Moon.

Not that I know anything about such things. Ahem...

'There is no physical, no spine, no scoliosis. Just Light and information. DO YOU *GET* THAT?!!!' he shouts to the audience.

Mesmerized, we all just nodded.

Holy shit. I sure as hell got it.

Ten minutes later, our grandmother began to stir and stagger to her feet, assisted by one of his Facilitators (senior staff). Before she's completely upright, Dr. Bartlett whirls her around and bends her over ass-out to the crowd. Unintentionally, I'm sure.

Roaring with laughter when he notices what the audience was laughing at, he explains that this posture is relevant (and useful), because she couldn't bend at the waist for years previously.

'Isn't that true, ma'am?' he asks her gently.

'Yes it is,' she squeaks dreamily.

'That feels good, huh? Better?'

'Si. Yes it does.' She was so cute you just couldn't stand it.

Then Dr. Bartlett lifts the back of her shirt again and scrapes down her spine with his thumbnail. *Perfectly straight.* You could see the winding red mark next to it where her spine used to be.

Half of us clapped madly while the other half just wore expressions of blank shock. It felt, right then, like my whole life had been leading toward this moment, this seminar, this teaching. I'm sure that everyone whom had spent a quarter of a million dollars on a formal education was feeling something too.

After demonstrating his all-patented, trademarked, copyrighted (with all rights reserved) Two-Point Technique on a few more attendees, he abruptly announces that we all were to stand-up and do it now. Everyone began to panic a little until a simple slide show with step-by-step directions showed us how to "do" Matrix Energetics.

He made it as simple as could be.

In fact, it's so easy that it's almost insulting to a practitioner with intricate trainings, but was so much more powerful.

It was like Craniosacral in that you used your faculty of observation to notice "stuck" areas, but instead of listening to held space in a physiological or anatomical model, you just connected what you noticed with a line, and let go.

Fuckin' ridiculous, right?

As Richard explains, if you shift a physical body part, then that's all you get and it probably has to follow the rules of Newtonian physics for what can happen, limiting the (observable) outcome.

However, if you shift a wave-front pattern or grid, through noticing what shows-up in the moment, then everything, even on a cosmic level, can change instantly and have exponential quantum repercussions.

Any two points that you'd notice would work too, whether on or off of the physical body. It was so natural for me that I began to assist others who were having issues with collapsing the wave.

The way that I performed the Two-Point technique began with the intent to notice the most jacked-up part of my partner's body, and my eyes would instantly snap there. Then touching that spot gently, I'd use my Craniosacral-developed intuition to pick my second point, and my hand would just float there (unless "there" was someone's breast or crotch, of course).

Then I connected these two dots (La la la la...Pee Wee Herman-style). Wave function activated. Check.

Then I moved my mind's attention to something else. *Anything* else.

This withdrawal of my focused attention to these connected nodal points of imperfection, *collapsed the line* (wave function) between the two dots *representing our observed measurement* of 'what doesn't feel right.'

Focusing the radar dish of our consciousness to another channel, so to speak, collapsed the wave. Dropping your awareness from the head into the field of the heart was another (and deeper) way of accomplishing this, according to Dr. B.

It was an amazing feeling. Participants were laughing, weaving, and falling-over everywhere. When the wave collapsed in the other person, you could feel it in your own being as well, and Dr. Bartlett called it "quantum entanglement." Our energy fields were actually One during this process, which summoned the justifiable concern about energetic transference ("bad" energy).

Not to worry, he mentions. The resonance can be broken with the act of intent, re-entering the intellect consciously, or by simply creating the rule that when this game is played, that you're not receptive to field influence.

What!? *We can make up our own rules?* I was used to consciousness systems that had pre-established do's and don'ts, as well as specific dynamics of how the energy does or doesn't respond. Matrix was so awesome because there were *no rules*. Only that Dr. Bartlett has created its framework so that it is non-harmful (very wise, I thought), with a promise to magically kick the ass of those who would try to use ME to nefarious ends.

Did I mention already that this guy was my hero? Well, I'll do it here. He's my hero (besides you, of course, Dad).

After returning from lunch, Dr. Bartlett informs us that it's time to take the play to another level by addressing the illusion of linear time. An Ascension Manual by Serapis gives a perfect model for this, but I'll merely redirect your mind to the earlier description of time as the circumference of one of our cuts in the orange. Viewed from a horizontal plane, it may look like a line, but is more akin to a circle viewed from the side.

Through this viewpoint and model, every point along this circle constitutes a "now" moment, where past, present, and future all coexist simultaneously (at least for this parallel reality...remember that the orange may be sliced in infinite ways).

Richard explains how our traumas and every other imperfect divergence experienced in this lifetime are strewn along this circle, creating our imbalances, poor habits, and pathologies. Theoretically (as it's *his* theory via Dr. Fred Alan Wolf) you could take a pattern or imbalance back through time (along the circle) and intend for the wave function to collapse whenever the "thing" or "incident" occurred.

He aptly called this approach, Time Travel Technique.

He made it, again, insanely easy. (Which was why so many folks had trouble with it at first. The left-brain loves complexity.) Basically, you find and connect your two points, ask the age of the person you're playing with, then count backward from the number they give you. The wave collapses when you reach the year when, *whatever*, happened.

Practice partners always looked surprised when we reached/connected to a year when "something" happened to them in life. They'd either already know of the mega-trauma that happened that year ('my parents got a divorce'; or 'I was sexually assaulted'; or the car crash, etc.), or sometimes they would take a minute, and remember things they'd forgotten for decades, the memory suddenly popping in their heads. Some folks would cry and process, others just weaved around in a bliss-state, or fell down.

Freaking powerful, magical stuff.

If your partner didn't want to reveal their age because they're insecure (no other reason), then you could just say or think, 'One year ago, two years ago, three,' etc. until you reached the year the imbalance was created. Then the pattern would collapse, huge change could be felt, and you could pick two new points. This all happened in a matter of seconds, too (though matter and seconds were barely acknowledged myths in this room!).

One lady I'd been practicing with said she had neck pain on and off for over a year; after getting back up off of the floor for the second time (she *really* went with it), smiled and informed me that all of her pain was gone.

Just like that.

It took maybe only a minute, and a near-miracle happened with me as the fulcrum or nexus. I couldn't believe how deeply the Universe had responded to my pleading prayers.

It dawned on me just how much change this Time-Travel Technique (™,©,®, patented, etc.) could render, from a theoretical perspective. If a pattern or trauma's energy could be shifted when brought back to its linear point of conception, and a new timeline is created as though the event had never happened (instantaneously), then the recipient's life could be exponentially altered in the "present" moment as that wave of different choice points rearranged itself holographically and linearly (as the brain interprets it).

Kind of sounds like the show Lost, right?

Basically, when the wave collapsed, it's like snipping the circle with scissors at that "point". A whole new arc of experience would instantaneously graft to the snipped piece, creating a completely new, though often-similar looking parallel reality, *minus* the crappy pattern (and resultant choices due to its happening).

You've seen a hundred movies where the main character's life is seen to be completely different in the absence of a car crash, or the 'What would my life have been like if _____ hadn't happened' or 'I chose *this* instead.' You get what I'm saying now? Like that.

As you might imagine, that has big implications not only for health, but holographic reality in general.

The first day of the seminar was winding to a close, and Dr. Bartlett announces that we had just enough time to discuss parallel realities and the Parallel Worlds Theorem. It sounded a bit like the orange-slice metaphor: That there were an infinite number of ways to slice a singular creation.

His point was, like the time-traveling metaphor, instead of finding a second point along the circle, that *any point within the orange* (where the event or condition *doesn't* exist) can be accessed and two-pointed, collapsing the wave-function into a more useful reality. A little like the show Quantum Leap portrayed.

Everyone was trying to not look too confused, but Richard rescued us from ourselves again, declaring the easiness of accessing parallel realities as cannon.

Basically (always basically), you picked your two points, connected them and inwardly acknowledged the intent to access a more useful parallel reality where the condition was healed or never existed in the first place. Then you counted, 'One parallel, two, three, four, five, etc. until you feel the collapse of the wave function. Mind-shaggingly easy.

When I got to my feet and began practicing, my brain simplified it for me. I found my first point on my partner's body, and then I imagined that my second point was on an iPod in my hand. The album covers were the parallel realities that I could flip into, so when I found one I liked, or felt good, I pushed the iPod button, and the wave function collapsed!

That was the first time that one of my points had become a holographic picture, what Dr. Bartlett termed an "archetype" like Jung's archetypes. He said that tomorrow, he would show us how interacting with holographic shapes and pictures with this Art could produce massive change in someone's life and take the sense of play to another level.

People everywhere were melting into the floor, the chair they were integrating in, or waving around in a bliss-state. Excited conversations were again breaking out when Richard announced that it was well past 5pm. It had felt like only an hour had passed, and at the same time like a week had gone by. Like in Peru.

He tried his best to vanish back to his hotel room, but was of course surrounded by guests who wanted clarity, or hoping for change in a physical condition. It made me respect Dr. Bartlett even more for patiently answering their questions, or emphasizing the importance of not "treating" a "condition or pathology." 'That only makes *that* field, energy, condition, etc. more real, and therefore more difficult to change. Don't see the problems, see solutions.'

I didn't envy him, the way everyone seemed to pull on his attention, but I guess that's the minor burden of spreading Light to so many, and from a whole new level. Call it "mastery in the marketplace," if you will, and I learned afresh what the meaning of those words embodied.

The doors to the conference hall opened one hour before the start time to give folks time to get seats quickly, and to practice the three techniques learned the day before. Everyone was Two-Pointing, Time-Traveling, and accessing Parallel Worlds, Universes, Realities, etc. to collapse the wave function. Many of us were exchanging ideas of how to use the approaches in new ways.

One that had occurred to me on the first day was to make "myself" one point, and to attach my other point to the end of an imaginary fishing pole (like the iPod idea). I could just cast my second point at whatever I wanted, and because the "fishing line" represented the wave function, whatever it landed upon would become an immediate measurement, and would automatically collapse the wave.

To give an example, when someone on stage was processing/integrating massive change and near drooling, Dr. Bartlett might shout, 'Now two-point into *her* to experience her shift!' I'd do my fishing pole technique and cast my second point into the person up there. When the wave collapsed, I could feel movements inside and around my body that matched the movements of the woman's body as it swayed or leaned.

Instantaneous empathy. (I coined it...dibbs! ®™)

The rock music was cued and Dr. Bartlett jumped onto the stage, coffee in hand. After settling down, he fields questions from the audience, clarifying intellectual concepts, or demonstrating the nuances of what he had taught previously.

He asks if anyone in the audience still doesn't get it. A few tentative hands go up. These people are all rounded-up like steers, and brought up onto the stage. The collective obstacle these few have is *over-intellectualization*. After Dr. B gives them a few consciousness redirections (they were noticing the wrong stuff), they all get it and the years and seriousness fall from their faces. They knock one another over, Two-Pointing or Time-Traveling with devastating effectiveness. Now we all can play.

Which was good, because playfulness, and regarding Matrix Energetics as play was key to accessing our deepest capacity of "let-go." Results were more arbitrary than connection and getting out of the way, but there appeared to be a correlation between one's capacity to do this and how much change occurred.

To illustrate the point, often Dr. Bartlett would work himself into near hysterics laughing on stage, and might pretend he had a bow and arrow, but when he fired it at the person on stage, *they would react as though a massive wave function had just collapsed, and often, so did they!*

Or he might reach over their head and declare, 'I see a multicolored, pulsating valve over your head. I'm gonna just turn it here…' Then as he turned the imaginary/hallucinated valve, the person on stage would weave around dreamily or collapse. He called this madness, Archetypes.

They didn't have to be Jungian archetypes, either. Dr. Bartlett's interaction with Superman during the patient visitation illustrates this. Any measured (congruently imagined) holographic shape or picture would work, like my "iPod" or "fishing pole."

An example he offered involved the scapula, or shoulder blade, that was essentially a triangle shape, and if viewed as a holographic triangle, every "conscious" interaction with that shape, such as rotating it, shrinking it, moving it in a direction (*whatever* occurred to you) would create correlative collapsed wave fronts in and around the "physical" person. The shoulder and person would move by moving the triangle shape.

This was a more concrete way to begin; imagining the interface of simpler geometries atop the physical parts of the body and interacting with them. When Dr. Bartlett did it, though, it made me realize how far we could take the Art.

He'd find his first point (usually) to begin, and he'd say that whatever showed-up next, he'd interact with and apply. If a dragon-skin belt with day-glow colors, a flaming buckle and feathers appeared in his mind's eye (as it did during this seminar), the next step would be to inwardly inquire how to apply, or dance with this archetype. If it occurred to him to apply it to an arm, like a tourniquet, then you do that. If it occurred to him to tie it around the waist, then he'd do that.

Dr. Bartlett emphasized that the stranger the thing that arrives, looks, or feels, the better. If it had been a regular black belt, it was more likely that the image was provided by the left-brain, not from the right, or unknown domain.

That's where the power was. You had to trust that whatever showed-up was the correct (archetypal) holographic representation of the first point, and dance with it. Every "move" created another dimension of change.

Richard was incredible. It was like he was using the cartoon physics of Roger Rabbit, hallucinating sledgehammers with flower patterns and smashing attendees with them, or imagining a paintball gun who's pellets contained quantum programs of Light, Love, and transmutation. As he pulled the trigger (once modifying the gun into a shot-gun for a *very* stuck shoulder), seminar participants waved and fell.

I saw him take a katana blade (samurai sword) in his hands and "decapitate" a woman on stage that had chronic neck pain and immobility, and she staggered backward as though a real sword had struck.

By the way, neck pain *gone*.

When we all rose to practice, everyone looked uneasy. He was so naturally trusting and clairvoyant; he looked like he was having so much fun on stage that we were all eager to succeed at this seeming impossible approach.

Now everyone, even the well educated, wanted to be as effectively crazy as Dr. B was.

Ironic, huh?

I found my first point on my partner, and softened my mind to allow a "something" to arrive. Just when I was about to panic that nothing would, all of a sudden, for whatever reason, one of the ballerina hippos in the movie Fantasia appeared, not only in my mind, but also over her right shoulder.

Okay. This is what Dr. Bartlett was lecturing on (I thought), but what next? As I made this inquiry, I watched said-tutued hippo do a leap off of her shoulder and dive into her right ear and head. I watched, tripping and amazed as the hippo began doing the breast-stroke through her cranial vaults and CS fluid.

Whoa (and of course, WTF)! I had just enough time to marvel at this as her body toppled-over onto the ground to integrate.

Okay, I thought, THIS IS AWESOME.

I took out my holographic fishing pole (because I had the notion to do it) and baited my "hook" with whatever arrived in my consciousness. A picture of the state of California would appear, I'd grab it with my fingers, put it on my hook and have a notion where to cast it at a particular spot. I'd cast California in, and her hip and leg would visibly rotate while feeling the sensation of the wave collapsing in myself.

It was crazy. To truly illustrate how cool this really was, at another seminar (because, of course, I went again and again) Dr. Bartlett was explaining how *any* holographic object, shape, or form could provide this function, because all points in creation are connected to every other point and all fields interpenetrated one another (according to the quantum physics model).

Basically, that by using your focus (intent), you could theoretically access the limitless power and information of the Zero Point Field (the Unified Field, or God) via the subconscious (ego) and superconscious (Soul) minds, as easily as pushing a button on a TV clicker.

For this example, because he was a big fan, he'd be accessing the many brilliant archetypes contained within the Potter series. WTF!

WTF!!!

In my book (*literally* in *my* book) Richard Bartlett is James Dean wrapped in the aura of Steve McQueen. So cool, ice cubes feel warm. Dude!

He borrows a ball-point pen from someone in the front row and asks the lady to come onto the stage. I could feel how stuck her hips and abdomen were from where I was sitting.

'So I'm going to access my wand here' he says, holding the pen/wand out for us to see. I could almost feel the pen become a wand and hallucinated flashes of it. Then when it looked like he felt ready, he pointed his wand at her abdomen and cried, 'Expelliarmus!'

Now, in the Potterverse (which is what Potter-nerds refer to as the parallel universe (slice) where there *is* an actual

English wizard school...I know that sounds certifiably insane, but watch enough Star Trek or talk to a quantum physicist and you may admit to its possibility), this spell's function is to disarm your attacker's wand. It was used in that reality to great effect by Barry, and perfectly explained by Dr. Dean-McQueen.

He reiterated that he incanted the first words that arrived once the pen became a wand and was accessing the physics of that parallel world. If he tried to "pick" a spell to "fix the problem," he'd already be limiting the depth of what could be accessed.

If the word "Bellisimo!" had arrived in his inner ear, he says he would have shouted that, because it would have come from his right brain and not left. The right brain accessed multidimensionality and then processes the data (or maps reality) linearly in the left. Remember that.

That's why the stranger the archetype looks, feels, or sounds, the closer to its undiluted origin in the right brain where it came from.

It doesn't get much stranger than a chiropractic/naturopathic doctor pointing a pen-wand at someone's abdomen in front of three hundred people and expect anything to happen, much less creating a healing response.

The lady toppled-over almost instantly.

When she got back to her feet, I could feel that the blockage was gone and her legs had rotated out (they were medially rotated or inwardly turned). He validated this, with her laughing hysterically, by rotating her completely liberated hips around forcefully like a hula dancer.

I was *losing my mind and geeking-out beyond repair.*

This healing miracle was brought to you by a Gary Potter spell.

If I were writing a graduate level thesis, this would be its cumulative moment. (I can stop watching T.V.! Yeaaaaaah! – sorry; obscure P.C.U. reference!) I now occupied a universe where I truly felt that *anything* could happen.

God I love my life!

Once we were all seated again, Dr. Bartlett led us into what is perhaps the most unique element of the Art that is Matrix Energetics, the 21 Frequencies.

One day, he says, his spiritual guides who help him with Matrix (like guardian angels) tell him audibly and loudly to grab pencil and paper, because they'd be downloading to him the unheard-of 21 Freqencies that govern healing and disease in the human body, and to please record what comes up.

I was forcefully reminded of the moments Neale Donald Walsch describes before he began recording his dialog with God for his amazing books (emphasis on **amazing**).

Revolutionary healing arts and sometimes religions can form that quickly. It just depends in those moments if you have the guts and wisdom to follow the heart and not the mind. This guide's voice was familiar and forceful enough for Dr. B to heed the request. He says that It had saved his life when he was a child.

For full details of what seamless guide communication can *really* be like, read Dr. Bartlett's first published work, of course titled, <u>Matrix Energetics: The Science and Art of Transformation</u>. *It's fucking mind-bending, by the way.*

So he, along with Dr. Mark Dunn and a few other clairvoyantly gifted people, examined and experienced the qualities, or personality, of every Frequency downloaded/channeled on that day. Their descriptions of how each one generally functioned were outlined in the manual, but Dr.

Bartlett wanted us to turn each one on and experience them for ourselves.

He mentioned that when his guides were downloading this information in him, they utilized a template, or energy program like a computer disk that had the information of the Frequencies in it. Using intention, Dr. Bartlett would likewise be creating a template for us (this process was uniquely different every time it showed-up, like a Dave song), and download the same information into we audience members as well.

This sounded a bit like an attunement to me, otherwise couldn't a person just Two-Point into the Field where Matrix Frequencies were, and just collapse the wave? This may be, at present, the only function within Matrix Energetics not described or taught through his two books.

If you don't already have them both, purchase them now. His newest offering is <u>The Physics of Miracles</u>. I feel like I'm experiencing controlled explosions inside my skull when I read it. They're going to change humanity for generations, like discovering the world isn't flat, or Tesla's utilization of alternating current.

After accepting a pyramid-shaped holographic construct that Dr. Bartlett had visualized, we placed them in our hearts and intended to activate the program. I slumped in my chair and everyone looked as though they were in deep meditation (which is really cool when a couple hundred people are doing it at one time!). When we all fully returned to our bodies, we were led by Dr. Bartlett in a group meditation, turning on each Frequency in turn, feeling the sensations, and writing notes on their many uses and functions.

We were asked to turn them on and off by visualizing a big control panel in front of us with twenty-one toggle switches. To turn them on, you simply flipped the switch with your mind or physical fingers. There was a dial on this panel that increased or decreased their flow.

Dr. Bartlett informs us all that we can put *anything* on this holographic panel, *any* energy, master, or archetype... *anything*. This really kicked ass to me as you might imagine. Like an iPhone with any application your mind could conjure. More on this later.

By the time we all paired-up, this time, everyone seemed to get it. Just like with Parallel Universes, we just connected our Two-Points, and thought, 'Frequency One, Two, Three, etc. until the wave function collapsed.

Sometimes a pattern would only partially collapse when the "correct" Frequency was selected, and would require another Frequency for complete resolution.

Dr. Bartlett told us that the Frequencies possessed multidimensional consciousness of their own, and we could trust that when we turned one on, it knew what to do. Richard credits Dr. Dunn's exponentially developed clairvoyant abilities to having meditated within each of them for only 30 seconds everyday. A little over ten minutes every day brought this consciousness-pioneer to the frontier of visionary exploration. Perhaps we should emulate him? I am.

So...Frequencies. Awesome.

Next, we began learning about Matrix Energetics Healing Modules, a concept developed by Dr. Bartlett and Dr. Dunn.

Like the holographic pyramid construct, a preconceived template with various Frequencies, angelic archetypes, medical strategies, sacred geometry relating to the Kabbalistic Tree of Life, etc. preprogrammed into it could be released into a person's energy field and activated, creating amazing changes.

One module, or program, might have as few as twenty individual functions.

Dr. Bartlett said that after hundreds of hours of guidance and meditation, he and Dr. Dunn created the original 30 Healing Modules, all of them highly powerful, self-intelligent, and self-upgrading. You could essentially count to the correct module (one, two, three, four, etc.) until you felt a shift in the held point, intend that it activate, and walk away.

Or, you held out your hand, "downloaded" the appropriate module for your partner, and when your hand filled with the energy of the module (or hallucinated a form), you could just toss the energy in and stand back.

Like an unfolding, activating computer program, you could witness the information working its way through their body, creating shift after shift in them. Richard even said that you could just download *whatever* information the subject needed for the 'highest change possible' onto a template, and then activate it. Then just let it go.

Sometimes the modules I'd pick would turn into an image in my hand, like a baseball or a futuristic mechanical insect. But once I placed it somewhere and activated it, I could just watch while multiple quantum wave fronts changed before my eyes.

Once while practicing, I created a full one-hour treatment of Craniosacral Therapy and Shamballa MDH into one module and tossed it to someone. They looked confused at first, then blissful, then sat down hard in their chair.

Pre-packaged quantum programs of limitless change, release, and expansion!

Alchemy and science together...and it's fun to realize this process is *real* and *actually happening*. It definitely was for the ecstatic quantum physicists, physicists, and engineers I talked to. Ditto for the housewives and medical professionals, faith healers and teenagers.

'Tomorrow's the big day though!' Dr. Bartlett exclaims before we part. 'Level 2 is what it's all about because we synthesize all that you've learned and take it to a whole new level. If you haven't signed-up for tomorrow, you should.'

Fifty people immediately rose from their seats and nearly trampled one another attempting to reserve their space.

I left mine, and the building, with a supreme sense of my environment's fluidity and malleability; how connected it was though attention and intention. I could barely wait for the following day, or to return to my "healing" practice.

By this time, every seminar participant had an auric atmosphere of youthful freedom and magical mischievousness. Every face shone with joy (especially once the coffee table had been set-up) and anticipation for whatever else we could possibly discover at this point. We'd already been turned inside-out, and our worlds flipped upside-down.

Gratefully.

After we'd been watered (or coffeed) we found our seats, sharing incredible stories with our neighbors about the many small (and often vast) miracles that had already happened. Arthritis that had vanished, carpal tunnel syndrome eradicated, low backs now ready for salsa lessons. How could this get better?

I love that question-mantra. Say it many times throughout your day if you wish to lead an amazing, Grace-filled life. Just saying...

Dr. Bartlett manifests in front of us all once more, conducting our enjoyment of morning rock music from the stage. Then he invited a few participants to share any healing stories or consciousness awakenings they might have experienced. One woman said she could see auras now. A man with a bulging disk in his low back was now pain-free.

Richard's face was alive with manic energy as he elaborated and clarified the finer points of what had been taught, making references to the Ascended Masters and ancient mystery schools that taught the art of self-transformation, or alchemy. WTF?!

As his spiritual teacher Elizabeth Clair Prophet had once channeled from Saint Germain, 'Alchemy is the

All-Chemistry of God' whose formulae could transform one's identification with the lead (karma filled) ego-self, into union with the gold of the Soul.

It sure felt like that was what we were experiencing during this seminar, but that knowing could only be birthed by experience, not postulation.

No one raised a hand to argue.

I *knew* we had the same alma mater!

For nearly three days now, everyone had noticed that Richard performed Matrix Energetics in a unique way. When he wasn't up to extraordinary antics, cartoonishly creating changes by playing with Archetypes, we'd witness him pick a point on the demo person's body, and with his other hand, would kind-of sweep the air in front of him with either his whole hand, or fingers, looking like he was playing "air piano."

When it looked like he'd find "something," whatever it was, he'd either grab it and let it go in their field, or the person would simply drop.

He finally explained what he was doing and why it took the technique of Matrix Energetics to an Art form.

Richard asked us all if we remembered the holographic panel with the toggle-switches, dials, and buttons that activated the Frequencies, modules, or anything else you chose to place there (metaphysical knowledge, medical procedures, spiritual energies, Masters, etc.) He and his staff actually created a page in the back of our manual folders as a visual example.

What he is doing, he says, is interacting with the information as though that panel was hovering in front of him, like a holographic computer interface. Like Tom Cruise's character utilizes in the movie Minority Report, as he sifts through the holographic pictures and info that the Pre-Cogs (psychic people who can see a murder happen before it does) dreams-up.

Except Dr. Bartlett's informational interaction and exploration is intended to created the highest transformational experience that is possible, not solving murders that haven't occurred yet.

Dr. Bartlett named this approach "Windows" (though it's far more Mac than PC!)

Before we even started the lesson, he made us hold up our right hands and solemnly swear aloud that this would be easy and that we'd be amazing at it. That neutralized our unspoken doubts that we could do as he did, and put our egos' in their place to receive new information.

He describes his favorite way of interacting with the Matrix Field as kinesthetic, or tactile. Feeling the sensations neurologically with his fingertips or hands is the deepest way he says that he connected with the Field.

He asks us to wave our right hand through the space in front of us. Just air. Then he requested that we imagine a set of holographic windows in front of us, like icons on a computer. Then, we were instructed to label the windows of information as Two-Point, Parallel Universes, Time-Travel, Archetypes, Modules, or any other possible field your right brain may inspire.

Then we held our hand up to where the windows were and felt the space for an "open" window. It was a trip to feel a cushiony barrier in the space in front of me if the second point wasn't the "icon" I was selecting (closed window). When your hand passed through an "open window," you accessed the energy and the wave function collapsed.

You could pull a holographic archetype out of the window and apply it to your partner or client. Sometimes, going through the window for Frequencies partially collapsed the wave of my partner, but then the picture of the Frequencies panel floated in front of me (as a sub-application). As I flipped-on the correct Frequency(s) the person collapsed to the ground. Trippy!

Each window entered opened a deeper aspect of the pattern to collapse and a deeper layer of the "icon's" programming information. When a "Done" window showed up, there was nothing left to do, and the session was complete. It even *felt* that way; I failed to notice another pattern to play with on my partner, or first point.

I realized quickly that I didn't have to use my hands or fingers either. As soon as a new window displayed itself, like Parallel Universes, I could intend to find the correct window instantly, or shuffle them like my (old-school) iPod with my mind. The wave collapsed, or a new set of options would arrive instantly when the correct "button" was pushed. I felt like I was in the movie Click.

You could customize you Windows Panel, also. I use Mac, so I visualized an iPhone/iPad with my Matrix Application Icons and tapping them with my fingers activated or accessed the energy.

It was incredible and ridiculous and the most powerful thing I had ever experienced.

Folks were holding one point with their hands, and groping at the space before them, looking shocked when their partners crumbled. The trick was to *really* experience what a closed window felt like, so it was obvious when your hand passed through an open window. Feeling the wave collapse, and your partner weaving about, provided secondary validation that you hadn't completely lost your mind.

It was comforting, at least, to be surrounded by two to three hundred people who seemed to be having the time of their lives losing theirs.

Throughout the day, Richard introduced us to amazing concepts, technologies, teachers, Masters, archetypes, and knowledge that we could apply to our "Matrix Quantum Computer."

I won't share those here...you'll just have to attend a seminar and receive these magical teachings for yourself. I will, however, explain the most powerful idea he shared, and why it makes Matrix Energetics the supreme healing/ transformational art in existence today.

Using Matrix, you can access *any* field, *any* energy, *any* knowledge (subconsciously) without having to have conscious understanding of them, or instruction in them. Just by Two-Pointing into its field. You could even access *future* systems that haven't been channeled or discovered yet! I loved that one.

Richard says that at one point in his practice, he had photographs all over his office of Ascended Masters and Jon of God who lives in Brazil (in my opinion the greatest healer on Earth). Any time he felt stuck with one of his patients, Dr. Bartlett says he'd imagine reaching into Jon's picture and pulling-out the energy of what he'd do were he present. Manifesting *miraculous* results.

I often do this now, as well as Two-Point into Dr. Bartlett's future conscious (and unconscious) understanding and ability to do ME. Dr. Dunn's clairvoyance. Niccolo Tesla's abilities with understanding physics. Saint Germain's alchemical knowledge.

It's like a skeleton key.

That's why I am declaring here that it is the Supreme Ultimate (so far). It's like purchasing one Application at the Mac Store that can *run or access any application ever created or will ever be created.*

Capiche?

Attending a Matrix Energetics seminar and reading Dr. Bartlett's books have brought my energetic and spiritual efficacy to undreamed-of levels. It's akin to receiving an invitation to reclaim the magic of Life we experienced in rare moments during childhood. It's the reclamation of your birthright and mastery as a conscious creative force in Source's infinite worlds of exploration.

Indeed, Level 3 of Matrix Energetics training is named Whizard Training...where the boundaries of quantum theory and mechanics blurs into the realms of humanity's cultural treasure troves of mysticism.

An invitation to magical being, of Soulful, magical play awaits even you.

Do you accept?

My prayer is that you reclaim the home in your heart, the wand in your mind, and the thirst for inner exploration.

Child of the Most High...Know *and Enjoy* Thyself!!

Thou Art That.

The embodiment of Love's magic. A quantum wizard.

Bibliography

Bartlett, Richard. *Matrix Energetics: The Science and Art of Transformation.* Hillsboro, OR; NY: Atria Books/Beyond Words Publishing, 2007.

Bailey, Alice A. *Ponder on This.* New York: Lucis Publishing Co., 1971.

Carr, Allen. *The Easy Way to Stop Smoking.* London: Penguin Books, 1987.

Castenada, Carlos. *The Teachings of Don Juan: A Yaqui Way of Knowledge.* Berkeley, CA: University of California Press, 1969.

Cooper, Diana. *A Little Light on Ascension.* Hollywood, CA: New Earth Publications, 1999.

Croudo, Sion. *A Success Story of a Single Parent: The Best Father - The Coolest Dad.* Philippines: Xlibris Co., 2009.

Dychtwald, Ken. *Bodymind.* New York, NY: Penguin Putnam Inc., 1977, 1986.

Eker, T. Harv. *Secrets of the Millionaire Mind.* New York: Harper Collins Publishers Inc., 2005.

Herbert, Nick. *Quantum Reality: Beyond the New Physics.* New York: Random House, Inc., 1985, 1987.

Hicks, Esther and Jerry. *Ask and It is Given: How to Manifest Your Dreams.* Carlsbad, CA: Hay House, Inc., 2004.

Grattan, Brian. *Mahatma I & II*. Sedona, AZ: Light Technology Communications, Inc., 1991.

Kaa, Sri Ram and Kira Raa. *Sacred Union: The Journey Home*. San Fransisco, CA: Robert D. Reed Publishers, 2003.

Kiyosaki, Robert T. and Sharon L. Lechter. *Rich Dad Poor Dad*. New York, NY: Warner Books, Inc., 1997.

Moore, Christopher. *Lamb: The Gospel According to Biff, Christ's Childhood Pal*. New York, NY: HarperCollins Publishers Inc., 2002.

Pearce, Joseph Chilton. *The Biology of Transcendence*. Rochester, VT: Park Street Press, 2002.

Ruiz, Don Miguel. *The Four Agreements: A Practical Guide to Personal Freedom, a Toltec Wisdom Book*. San Raphael, CA: Amber Allen Publishing, 2001.

Scheinfeld, Robert. *Busting Loose From the Money Game*. Hoboken, NJ: John Wiley and Sons, Inc., 2006.

Stone, Joshua David. *The Complete Ascension Manual: How to Achieve Ascension in This Lifetime*. Flagstaff, AZ: Light Technology Publishing, 1994.

Stubbs, Tony. *An Ascension Handbook*. Lithia Springs, GA: World Tree Press, 1991.

Tachi-ren, Tashira. *What is Lightbody?*. Lithia Springs, GA: World Tree Press, 1990.

Tompkins, Peter and Christopher Bird. *The Secret Life of Plants*. Harper and Row, Publishers, Inc., 1973.

Urantia Foundation. *The Urantia Book*. Chicago, 1955.

About the Author

Joshua Ramay is an energy healer in San Diego, California. Following a spiritual awakening, Joshua's driving passion in life and healing philosophy have revolved around energy— not simply the fabric and expression of all reality but also the entirety of our experience as beings of Love and Light. This is especially true when he's with his amazing, wonderful, and Goddessly wife Abby.

Printed in the United States
By Bookmasters